"*Vector to Destiny*, by George W. Kohn, is now the trifecta of books on my recommended list. It is a compelling collar-grabbing page-turner by an expert who is a masterful storyteller. The author is overly modest and quick to point out his shortcomings as a farm boy taking childish risks with farm machinery, as a student, and beyond. He has highs and lows, flaws, successes, and failures. The author weaves a brilliant story you don't want to miss. From the beginning of the book, the young George will capture your heart and pull you into his world. The characters come to life and become people you know and care about—you are there with them. And you are right there in the cockpit of the F-4 Fighter with Lieutenant Kohn. You will cheer and laugh and, at times, choke-up with tears. I did not want the story to end, but I don't think I am giving anything away when I say the ending will leave you with a satisfied nod. *Vector to Destiny* deserves a broad readership, and I look forward to the movie." —*Nick Chiarkas, author of the award-winning novel,* **Weepers**

"I really like the book . . . it was both attention grabbing and captivating . . . I couldn't wait to finish it and when I did, I wished that there was more—not that George's story was incomplete, but he writes so well that I was wishing there were more chapters. Now, just to be fair, the content was right in my wheelhouse—I grew up working on my uncle's dairy farm and I have always held a deep and abiding respect for the military, especially Air Force (my eldest son was in the reserve). So the author had me from the start on this one."
—*Pastor Nathan Krause*

"**You are there!** George captures a piece of history from a participant's viewpoint and takes you right into the action. Feel the tension as you dive into enemy gunfire on bombing runs or as you listen to the enemy rocket attacks when you're on the ground. This book made me glad I flew the RF-4 instead of the F-4E." —*Gordon Savage, Vietnam RF-4 pilot, author of* **Peacemaker, Teleportal** *and* **Teleportal: Damage Control**

Vector to Destiny
Journey of A Vietnam F-4 Fighter Pilot

by George W. Kohn

© Copyright 2020 George W. Kohn

ISBN 978-1-64663-157-5

Published by

◤ köehlerbooks™

3705 Shore Drive
Virginia Beach, VA 23455
800-435-4811
www.koehlerbooks.com

VECTOR

TO

DESTINY

Journey of a Vietnam F-4 Fighter Pilot

George W. Kohn

VIRGINIA BEACH
CAPE CHARLES

This book is dedicated to my dearest sister, Delores, who left this earth way too soon and for all the wrong reasons, and to Ma and Dad for putting up with an adventuresome son. I would especially like to remember those who gave their all for the benefit of both the grateful and the ungrateful. May your sacrifice be forever revered in the annals of history.

TABLE OF CONTENTS

PREFACE

After many years of thinking about why things happened in my life, it was time to put thoughts into words. The central character in this story was one determined kid. I was that kid and there were many obstacles to overcome in order to reach my lofty goals.

My future as a farmer was all planned for me until something happened to change it. I experienced thrills, danger, and humiliation while traversing an exciting adventure through life. Many of my escapades were out of character for me, but they were pathways to a destiny. Despite some limitations, I eventually achieved my desired success.

Please enjoy my story, maybe entertain some new thoughts, and learn a few things along the way. Forgive me if some information is not precise but memories fade over time. And, if you would like to contribute your life's adventures to my next stab at writing a book, please email me at the address at the end of this story.

Special thanks,
George

PART ONE

THE FARM

My early Wisconsin wintry mornings began with Ma yelling up the stairway to my bedroom in our old farmhouse.

"George, George, it's time to get up."

I considered Ma's first call to be just a friendly wake-up reminder and I could still get a few more minutes in bed. She, however, was expecting me to immediately roll out of my warm bed, get dressed, and get down to the barn to help feed the calves and milk the cows before going to school. Early morning chore duties were intended to prepare me for someday taking over the family farm. I was the only son, and I suspected that the reason for my existence was that Dad needed a son to carry on the family farming tradition. The farm was the original Kohn homestead from when our ancestors emigrated in the 1800s from Germany. My father was so intent on me taking over the farm that he even named me George, which means earth-worker or farmer. I had other ideas.

I learned that I could enjoy at least ten more minutes of tranquility under the thick blankets on my nice warm bed. Ma was busy getting the fires burning in the basement furnace to get some heat in the house. On her second call though, I sensed an increasing urgency for me to get out of bed. She dragged out pronunciation of my name and her voice was a few decibels higher.

"George! George! Get out of that bed *right* now!"

Even her raised voice did not motivate me to just throw back the covers and expose my nearly naked body to the frosty bedroom temperatures. I justified more bedtime by assuming that her second call was only intended to agitate me so that I would not fall back asleep.

The only heat in my bedroom radiated from bricks in a chimney built into one of the inside walls of the house. The bricks were warm when hot smoke rose through the chimney. If there was fire in the furnace, there was smoke going up the chimney and I got heat. Otherwise, the temperature in my bedroom closely matched the frigid outdoor temperature. Ma stoked the fire in the furnace with a good supply of wood before going to bed at night, sometimes adding coal to keep it burning longer. The fire quickly burned through the fuel so that by early morning, the entire farmhouse was frigid until Ma restarted the fire.

Our old two-story farmhouse was built in the 1800s, and even though it lacked some comfort features, like continuous central heat, I found it to be somewhat accommodating and intriguing. A heavy iron grating in the downstairs living room floor above the furnace was the sole outlet of heat from the fire below. This living room was our relaxation area where we spent our free time after chores at night by reading, talking, and playing games—that is, until we got a television. Ma was in command of the house and seemed constantly busy with keeping the fires burning, cooking, and housekeeping, plus helping with outdoor farm work. She kept our old farm home in immaculate condition. She even hired a painter to detail the wainscoting in the living room with an artistic woodgrain appearance.

A kitchen off the living room had a large dining table that seated eight or more people. Males were considered the head of household, so Dad always sat at the head of the table, with Ma on his right and my sister Eunice across from Ma. I sat at the other end of the table, facing Dad. An iron cookstove in the kitchen had a flattop surface and a thick glass oven door. Once a week Ma baked bread, and I tried to be there when she took it out of the oven so I could inhale its aroma, slice off the end of the loaf, and spread it with a big slab of butter. It was real butter, not the fake stuff; margarine was illegal in Wisconsin. The kitchen stove had a water reservoir on one end that provided hot water to wash the dishes. I got stuck with helping my sister wash and dry supper dishes unless I could find some excuse that my help was needed elsewhere. Eunice often tried the same excuse.

An entryway shanty attached to the kitchen served as the main entrance into the house from outdoors. One of my hated jobs was to carry in wood from an outdoor woodshed and stack it in the shanty. It was fuel for the fire in the cookstove. Outside, a few feet from the shanty was a tall wood pole, on top of which was perched a cast iron farm dinner bell. Stamped on the bell was the year 1886. It had been used in the old days to summon the farm help to come out of the fields to eat dinner. I sometimes jerked its chain because I liked to make noise.

The farmhouse had no indoor plumbing. There was a two-holer outhouse for Ma and Eunice to use just a few feet away from the house. I rarely used it, preferring to do my thing into the gutters in the warm barn versus using the freezing outdoor toilet in the winter. Anyway, the oat straw used for the cow's bedding material was a gentler wipe than a page out of the Sears catalogue.

On Ma's third call, the tone of her voice and the sound of my full name indicated that I had stalled in bed about as long as I could.

"George William Kohn! Get out of that bed right now or I'm *coming up there!*"

I was not sure what would have happened if she did come up to my room, but I was not about to find out. I recognized that I better get out of bed and enter the real world of a farm kid. I grabbed my socks, t-shirt, blue jeans, and flannel shirt off the rocking chair in the corner and scampered across a cold wood floor to the stairway. I jumped down the stairs with my clothes in hand. By now, Ma's hot wood fire was starting to crackle in the cast iron furnace in the basement. A hint of heat was rising through the metal grating in the living room floor, so I stood directly on it to get into my cold clothes. My high-top shoes and fleece-lined coat were in the kitchen behind the wood cookstove that Ma had also fired up. My winter coat also served as a bed for our farm dog, Snooks, so he kept it warm for me throughout the night.

Having procrastinated in bed meant that I now had to hurry down to the barn. If I showed up late to do my chores, I could expect a verbal reprimand from Dad.

"Du bist du freak tuf yung-en"

I wondered what that meant in English, but it did not matter. I suspected from the tone of his voice that he was probably scolding me in German. Dad spoke fluent German as a second language even though he only had a fourth-grade education. Possibly, those German-sounding words did not mean a thing and he just made them up to vent his frustration with a half-asleep kid.

Our cattle barn was the warmest place on the farm those wintery mornings because it trapped the body heat from the fifty or so dairy cows. It was built in the 1800s on a fieldstone foundation, so it had excellent insulation properties. Attached to the front end of the barn was a sloping roof, under which there was a milk shed, feed storage area, and the entryway to the barn.

As I slid apart the big barn doors just far enough to squeeze my skinny body between them, a blast of aromas and odors hit me in the face. The sileage that we fed to the cows had a pleasant fermented corn smell. Ground oats had sort of a honey aroma with a hint of baked bread. It was sprinkled on top of the sileage. Cows loved it so much that when one finished her helping, she tried to stretch her neck to steal some from an adjacent cow. Sileage and grain were treats to encourage cows to give more milk. When they finished this good stuff, we forked dried grassy smelling alfalfa hay into the manger in front of them so that they had something to chew their cud on throughout the day.

As the cows were milked, the buttery aroma of warm milk wafted throughout the barn. The milk was emptied into milk cans that were later placed in a cold-water tank in the milk shed. A little warm milk was poured into a small dish in the barn to keep the kitties happy.

The barn also had the eye-stinging odors of cow manure and urine. After being tied up in their stanchions, each cow filled the gutter behind them with nearly seventeen gallons of their excreta per day. Unless it was beastly cold outdoors, after the milking in the morning, cows were let out of the barn into a barnyard so that we could complete the daily ritual of cleaning the gutters and refreshing their bedding material. When the cows were let back into the barn, they paraded down an aisle that had been freshened with a sprinkling of powered white lime. Each cow had a designated place in the barn. They stuck their head through a stanchion which I gently closed around their neck to keep them from wandering around the barn when unattended. In front of the cow was a manger for their food, and a water cup that they could fill by pressing their nose down against a float-type screen. When they had their bellies full of food and water, there was a thick bed of fluffed up straw for them to lay on.

Other than those annoying wake up calls, I considered the farm to be pleasant and peaceful early in the morning. Cows occasionally mooed, pigs squealed, ducks quacked, chickens cackled, and roosters crowed. The milking machines in the barn had a sucking and releasing rhythm when they were used to extract milk from the cow's udders. I managed to convince Dad that cows gave more milk if there was music for them to listen to, so I got a radio and cranked it up full volume to '50s rock and roll. Dad would have preferred big band music, but he made sacrifices to keep me happy.

One morning as we were doing our chores in the barn, an earth vibrating, thunderous boom rattled the thick stone walls of the barn and drowned out all the other sounds. It startled both the animals and us. Cows raised their heads, Snooks barked, even the kitties scampered to a safe hiding spot. Dad, Ma, and I ran outside fearing that something had exploded on the farm. There was no evidence of smoke or damage. The boom sounded like thunder, but there were no thunderstorms in sight. Could it be that we were under attack from the Russians? Both the United States and Russia were developing nuclear weapons. In the 1950s, the rhetoric between the two countries was heated, so there was cause for concern. Other locals were also startled by that sound, and the local newspaper reported that they got many phone calls to see if they had any information about the source of it. The newspaper ran an article in its next edition.

The US Air Force was conducting testing missions with its new supersonic B-58 bomber, called *the Hustler*. Their route took them directly over our farm. They were flying faster that the speed of sound, and the sound energy from their shock wave created a startlingly loud boom. The flights became frequent. I looked up to the sky each time to try to spot those airplanes. They were so fast that by the time I finally saw them by tracking their noise, they were already beyond me and all I could see was a speck ahead of their contrail. I tried to visualize the excitement that those pilots must experience strapped inside those airplanes as they streaked across the sky. If the Air Force needed an effective method for soliciting interest in its military might, those loud, high speed B-58 jets served that purpose.

The farm environment allowed me to challenge myself, sometimes pushing my abilities beyond the extreme. Full milk cans weighed about fifty pounds. They had handles on the side near the top so we could lift them in and out of the cooling tank. A milkman picked up the milk cans each morning and transported them to a farmer-owned cheese factory cooperative about a mile down the road. I admired the tall muscular milkman for his ability to simultaneously pluck two cans of milk from the tank by their handles, carry them to his truck, and hoist one of the full cans up onto the high bed of the milk truck without setting the other can down. I was just a skinny, five foot, eight-inch tall kid, but I had developed a muscular build from slinging hay bales, pitching sileage, shoveling manure, and lifting five-gallon buckets of swill to slop the hogs. I was determined to prove to this milkman, and to myself, that I could do the same thing as he did. First, I watched closely how he did it. Then, when he was right behind me and watching, I decided to try it. I could either look manly, or I could look like a weak fool. I pounded on the can covers with my fist to be sure they fit snuggly into the neck of the can, as I did not want to spill milk all over the ground if I failed. I used the can in one hand like a counter-balancing pendulum. I got the can in my other hand swinging back and forth a couple of times. Then, on one of the upswings, I got my knee behind it and gave it a hearty push up into the truck. The milkman had pretended like he was superman straight out of the comics. I revealed that it was more about technique than it was brawn.

A forty-foot tall cement silo was attached to our barn. It was filled with chopped corn that was blown into it through a pipe hooked up to a sileage blower. Every fall, the end of the blower pipe had a spout that had to be draped over the top rim of the silo through a slit in the tin roof. My job was to scale the outside of the silo by progressively grabbing the wire rungs cemented into the side and climbing to the top. At the top, I had to thread a rope through a wooden wheel pulley. One end of the rope was fastened to the spout end of the blower pipe laying on the ground. The other end of the rope was attached to our tractor. As the tractor was driven forward, the spout end of the pipe was hoisted up the side of the silo. I liked danger and decided to play up my job since I knew that Ma was watching. When I got to the top of the silo, I draped one leg over the top rung of the ladder, leaned back and used both of my hands to thread the rope through the pulley. I could almost hear Ma gasping.

The farm consisted of 160 acres with several outbuildings. A machine shed, granary, corn crib, and chicken coop were situated between the house and barn. Behind them, I could see off in the distance a clearly visible steeple and cross on a church that my great grandfather had helped to build after his arrival from Germany in the mid 1800s. It was visible for miles around and was obviously situated on that hill as a reminder that religion was a central bedrock principle for the community. It was close enough to our farm that, on a calm day, I could hear the church bell tolling. Ma and Dad made sure that I attended that church on a regular basis to be indoctrinated into religion. They made me attend Sunday school and catechism classes. Some of the bible stories were interesting, but the preacher's long boring sermons during church services made my mind wander into never-never land, dreaming about what I could do to live an exciting and adventurous life.

The numerous tasks on the farm were generally boring, but some generated my curiosity. Freezing and thawing winter temperatures forced stones in the field to the surface, so Dad and I had to walk the fields in the spring to pick up the stones so they would not damage our farm implements.

Occasionally we would spot an arrowhead. Various Menominee tribes had inhabited the area before my ancestors. Over the years, Dad had accumulated a cigar box full of colored arrowheads. One time I even found a square-shaped axe head, with a wide, thick poll that tapered down to a rather dull cutting edge. It was easily identifiable as an axe used by the natives because of the indented groove around the stone about halfway up from the cutting edge where it would have been tied to a handle.

A neighbor's farm just across the road had an elongated mound of dirt that Dad told me was an indigenous effigy mound, built in the shape of an animal. Neighboring kids and I were curious about its contents, but we had been taught to respect it as a sacred burial site. Dad told stories about Menominees coming to our farmhouse in the winter to beg for food. Grandpa Kohn gladly obliged by giving them meat, milk, and bread. I always wished that I could have met them, but they had already moved out of the area when I was a youngster.

A large accumulation of various sized stones from many years of field collection were piled near the bottom of the cow lane. Since all of Ma's meals were made in her kitchen, one day I decided it would be fun to do something different and build a bonfire to grill hot dogs. I organized some of the smaller stones into a burn pit, added dried leaves and twigs and started the fire with gasoline. I cut a long branch off a willow tree, sharpened the end of it with my jackknife and jabbed a hotdog onto it. I cooked it over the fire till it was nearly burnt and took a bite out of it. It tasted like gasoline. Even Snooks would not eat it.

Our farm had productive crop land, a wooded area, cow pasture, and a soggy swamp area. The swamp area was frequently waterlogged. Bogs stuck up above the water and I could skip across them without getting my feet wet. In the spring, local sportsmen brought baby pheasant chicks to the farm and released them into this swamp. They fed off Dad's field crops during the summer and became targets for shotguns in the fall.

Hickory trees in the woods were home to abundant squirrels and there was a plentiful supply of food for them. They got most of the nuts before Ma could collect them in the fall, but they left a few so she could make her hickory nut pies. I tried to control the squirrel population by hunting them with my .22-caliber rifle, but they were smart and hard to hit. They scampered around to the opposite side of the tree, then peeked around it like they were playing a game with me. Those rodents obviously did not understand that I was not trying to play a game; I was trying to shoot them.

RISK VERSUS REWARD

Growing up on a farm presented many dangers, a few rewards, and almost nothing to enhance my social maturation. I had no siblings close to my age, so I had to find ways to entertain myself. Dad had a Farmall C tractor that I was expected to drive at the age of eight in order to feed the pigs—one of my regular chores. I saw the tractor as a gasoline engine-powered toy, even though it was a heavy cast-iron farm machine. It had a tricycle axle, with the two front steerable wheels spaced close together; the rear wheels were spread about five feet apart. A three-speed transmission was engaged by a lever shift handle actuated by the driver's left hand. Two foot-actuated brake pedals controlled their respective left or right rear wheel. For farming operations, individual main wheel-braking was important to lock a rear wheel in place so you could make tight turns when using the tractor in the fields.

This tractor was used on our farm for a variety of tasks. For feeding the pigs, I used it to pull a wood sled-type stoneboat. Two fifty-five-gallon barrels were positioned on it, and they were filled with swill. Swill was made from whey, which was a leftover liquid from the process of making cheese with milk from our cows. The milkman offloaded the whey into the barrels when he picked up our milk. Dad added some ground corn and powdered nutrients into the whey to make it into swill. Pigs loved this stuff and I must admit that the warm yeasty smell of the whey combined with the fresh baked cornbread aroma from the ground corn almost made me hungry. I hooked a chain attached to the front of the stoneboat to a clevis hitch pin on the back of the tractor, then dragged it across the ground down to a pig trough in the barnyard below the barn. The pigs usually recognized the sound of the tractor coming as time to eat, but sometimes I had to get their attention by banging an empty five-gallon pail against the wood fence and hollering, *Sue-eee, sue-eee, su-eee, su-eee!*

Pigs disregarded all social graces when it was time to eat. They came running to the trough, snorting, squealing, pushing, and shoving. I scooped the swill out of the fifty-five-gallon barrels with a pail and dumped it into a long wooden trough. The big 500-pound mama sows got the first slop and the smaller pigs at the end of the trough had to wait for whatever remained of the swill to flow down to their end of the trough. When the big sows had their bellies full, they waddled back to their mud hole, then I dumped the remainder of the swill into the trough so that the little ones got some food too.

One wintry day after feeding the pigs, I got the brainy idea to use the tractor for a stunt just to see what would happen. The farm driveway was about 200 feet long and extended from the farm buildings to County Highway G. In the winter, the farm driveway often got icy after a snow or ice storm. I got a running start in second gear on a bare gravel area by the shed and shifted into third gear to speed up toward the end of the driveway. On a patch of ice, I cranked the steering wheel hard left, but nothing happened because the front wheels had no traction. So, I stomped the left brake down, which locked the left wheel in place. The tractor spun around in a tight 360-degree turn. I was proud of myself for figuring out how to do some sort of tractor wheelie if you can call it that. However, I did not account for the possibility that there may have been little patches of gravel sticking up through this clear ice. If the tractor tires had hit a patch of that exposed gravel, the sliding motion would have abruptly halted and the tractor would have flipped. Nearly everyone who ever ended up underneath an 1,800-pound farm tractor was severely injured or crushed to death. I got to thinking about that eventuality and never tried that stunt again. Divine intervention may have prevented bad results from my dumb maneuver.

The animals on the farm required lots of feed. Summertime was harvest time to store up feed for the winter. I attached a sickle bar mower to a tractor to cut alfalfa in the field for hay. After a couple of days to dry, Dad and I baled the hay and hauled it back to the barn. The upper level of the barn served as storage for hay. An elevator conveyed the bales from the wagon up into the hay mow (rhymes with cow) via a chain mechanism that was driven by a power takeoff shaft, or PTO, from the tractor. The shaft was inserted into a round-toothed sprocket at the base of the elevator. My job was to climb a wood ladder permanently affixed to a hand-hewn round pole upstairs in the barn and neatly stack the bales in the mow after they dropped off the end of the elevator.

One day, Ma and Eunice were on the hay wagon handing the bales to Dad, who was standing on the ground and loading them onto the elevator. Dad wore bib overalls, which were not always in the best of condition. I heard a loud scream from Ma.

"*Help! Help!*"

Forgetting about the ladder, I jumped out of the mow, about twenty feet down, into some loose hay on the barn floor. A tatter from Dad's overalls had gotten wrapped around the spinning elevator sprocket and started to rip a piece off his overalls. Dad was struggling to free himself, but the tatter was twisting and turning and forming into a rope. It would not tear off, so Dad was struggling to get out of his overalls. His arms were pinned against his body, and he had no way to free himself. The remnants of his overalls were twisting like a tourniquet around his chest. Air was being squeezed out of his lungs, and he was gasping. He was reaching the point of incapacitation. When I got there, Ma had already taken immediate action to shut off the tractor and to start cutting off his overalls with a jackknife that she took out of his pants pocket. When we got him free, Dad laid unresponsive on the ground. Ma was crying; the three of us all feared the worst. My mind was helter-skelter. I did not know what to do, except to say a silent prayer.

Lord, please let Dad be okay.

Possibly, Ma and my sister were doing the same thing. We loved Dad. Our family love was evidenced by a calm demeanor and with decency and respect toward each other. While my family rarely showed visible affection, like hugging or kissing, at a time like this I just wanted to lay down beside his body and give Dad a big hug. Thankfully, he recovered after his normal breathing resumed and I could enjoy him for many more years.

Ma's dad was Grandpa Wick. He sold his farm and moved to town, as many retired farmers did in those days, but farming was still in his blood so he occasionally came out to Dad's farm to help. Driving a tractor was second nature for him. Grandpa and I needed to hitch a twenty-foot long flatbed farm wagon to the Farmall C to haul some straw in from the field. The tongue bar on the wagon needed to be hooked into a drawbar on the back of the tractor. The tractor and wagon were hitched together by dropping a pin through a hole in the wagon tongue and into a corresponding hole in the drawbar. To speed things up, if two people were present, one would hold up the tongue on the wagon while the other backed up the tractor.

The Farmall C had a clutch pedal next to the brake pedals that you needed to push forward with your left foot to shift gears from first, to second, to third, to reverse, or into neutral. When you wanted to back up slowly, you slipped the clutch by letting it out part way to control the speed of the tractor.

Grandpa hopped on the tractor, started it up, shifted it into reverse, and slipped the clutch to slowly back it up toward the wagon. I held up the wagon tongue, ready to drop the pin through the two holes when they were aligned. Slowly, the tractor rolled back to the wagon. I was standing parallel to the inside of the five-foot tall solid rubber rear tractor tire. A fender was installed over the tire to keep dirt from flying into the face of the driver when doing field work. The soles of Grandpa's shoes were a little wet from walking in the dewy grass that morning. Grandpa's foot slipped off the clutch and the tractor suddenly lurched backward. I got pinned between the tire and the fender. I yelled,

"*Stop, stop!*"

Grandpa got the tractor's momentum stopped by stomping on both the clutch and the two brake pedals. He tried to free me by shifting into first gear and moving the tractor forward. The forward rotating tire only pulled me further into the narrow space between the tire and the fender. When he got it stopped, I was eventually able to wiggle my body free, and I dropped out onto the lawn in lots of pain.

Ma must have heard me yelling and looked out of the house to see what was happening. Seeing me writhing on the lawn, she immediately rushed to the phone to call Doctor Sharp. The phone was a hand crank type with a candlestick receiver and a microphone built into a wall box. It was on a party line, so any time you picked up the receiver, you could hear the conversation between other people that were currently using the line. I am sure that Ma's conversation went something like this.

"Please get off the line so I can call Doctor Sharp for an emergency."

The other people on the line knew Ma, so they, of course, willingly complied.

"Operator, please connect me to Dr Sharp immediately."

A telephone switchboard operator in our hometown inserted a plug into a receptacle that rang Dr. Sharp's number. Other people on the party line were nosy, especially if there was an emergency, so they probably listened in.

"Hello, Dr Sharp, my son is hurt; he got wedged between a tractor tire and the fender. He is laying on the lawn in lots of pain. Can you please hurry to the farm?"

Doctor Sharp made house calls, so he rushed to the farm and examined me. I had no broken bones, just skin rubbed off and a lot of bruising. All I needed was a little horse salve with some bandages on the wounds, plus some time in bed to rest. It was not how I had hoped to get more time in bed.

In this small town, word spread fast. Nosy people who listened in on Ma's phone call later jammed the switchboard to spread the word that I got hurt in a tractor accident. Several versions of the accident were created, with each story getting progressively worse. Ma started getting calls with offers of sympathy.

GOOD EATING,
BAD RESULTS

Ma was not just a good cook; she was a great cook and she had the finest ingredients with which to create her recipes. Dad designated one steer early on in its life to be the source of meat for our family. It was butchered around one year of age after it attained a weight of about 1,000 pounds. It was a half breed cross between a Holstein and an Angus. Dad fed it a diet rich in corn, grain, and hay to make sure its meat was tender and flavorful. He even put some sweet-smelling molasses in the ground feed to enhance the flavor for the steer.

Dad raised Hampshire pigs to sell as a source of farm income. These pigs had a black colored body with a white stripe that ran from one front leg across its back and down the other front leg. Dad raised pigs from birth until they were ready for market. His pig herd started with five or six fully grown female sows that he had selected for producing maximum piglet output. The best sows had litters of ten to twelve piglets. A good sow needed to have enough teats for each of the piglets to suck on. I used to snicker when city folks came to the farm and referred to them as *teats*. I tried to act like I did not know what they were talking about.

"Oh, you must mean *tits*."

If a sow only produced five piglets it would be destined for market; twelve piglets and it was retained for next year's breeding cycle. Little piglets were cute, but I learned early on to be cautious around a mama's babies. A sow pig was very protective of her babies and could run anywhere from fifteen to twenty miles per hour and attack you. I was no match in speed nor strength for confronting an angry 500-pound sow. I knew however, that a mama pig could not jump a fence like I could, so it was fun to sneak up on her, cuddle one of her babies in my arms when she was not looking, jump across the fence and pet the baby for a while. I would return the baby to her mom before she knew it was missing.

Butchering day was a big event at the farm, involving four neighbors who assisted with the slaughter. All animals at our farm were humanely killed—although the steer would probably not have considered it as very humane. A rifleman raised his .30-30 and fired a bullet between the steer's eyes. The steer immediately dropped dead to the barn floor. The carcass was rolled onto the stoneboat that was dragged to the front lawn. A rope-operated block and tackle winch was attached to a large oak tree limb in the front yard. It was used to hoist the carcass by its rear legs so that it could be gutted, skinned, and quartered. Quartering made it manageable for transport in Dad's pickup truck to a meat locker, where it would be cut and wrapped into packages of steaks, chops, loins, roasts, and ground hamburger.

Piglets matured fast, and by butchering time they weighed about 150 pounds. On butchering day, two unlucky pigs were randomly selected from Dad's herd of fifty or so swine on the farm. Pigs were shot with a revolver, bled, and dipped in hot steaming water to scald the hide so that a scraper could be used to remove the hair. This was a busy time for Ma as she heated up the wood-fired stove in the kitchen and melted some butter in a cast iron skillet to fry up the pig brains, which we ate on butchering day. They tasted delicious—if you could get past the idea that they were brains. I mentioned to my sister that eating them made me smarter, but I do not think that I convinced her.

Ma filled a big pot in the kitchen sink with water and soaked the pig's feet. After a few days, she cooked them on the stove for several hours in a vinegar and spices brine, and then stuffed them into mason jars for

GEORGE W. KOHN 19

later snacking. She boiled the pig's head, minus the eyes, and made head cheese by adding the head meat into a mixture of vinegar and gelatin. The heart and tongue were pickled in some type of vinegar solution. Ma and Dad liked those sour tasting German recipes; I could not stand the taste of those vinegary concoctions. Blood and liver were made into sausage that was smoked in our stone-walled smokehouse next to the farmhouse. I could not stand that stuff either. The intestines were soaked, salted, and dried and used for making summer sausage. The sausage was made with ground beef and pork plus several other ingredients. Ma fried some after all the ingredients were combined before it was stuffed into the casings, and it was delicious. Not much of butchered animals was wasted. Ma used to jokingly brag that she used everything from the pigs except the squeal.

A typical meal when guests visited the farm was steak or pork chops, homegrown potatoes, sweet corn, and canned cherries—the ones that Ma canned—and of course, homemade bread. The steak was so tender that it could be cut with a fork. Ma always fried steaks on the wood-fired stove since it was her only medium for cooking. Ma and Dad did not believe in using charcoal grills. There were three square meals a day—breakfast, dinner, and supper—with nearly all the food coming from the farm except for a few items, such as Wheaties cereal in the morning. Even sugar for the cereal came from sugar cane that Dad grew for a processing facility about one-half mile up the road. In the morning, Ma ladled pure cream off the top of the cans of milk to pour on our cereal.

I never fully appreciated Ma's delicious meals since that was all I had to eat, except for school lunches or a holiday meal at Grandma Wick's. Her good food should have made me a healthy young lad. Instead, I had routine bouts of tonsillitis, colds, the flu, and lots of pains. Visits to the doctor were frequent and I hated them because I always seemed to end up getting a shot. I had lots of pain in my legs, which was especially concerning to Ma and Dad. There were high incidences of polio, for which there was no cure. Some youngsters were permanently paralyzed, or they needed to wear leg braces for the rest of their life. Pictures of children in iron lungs were terrifying. On one visit to Dr. Sharp, I saw him motion for Ma to follow him into an adjacent room. I could overhear what they were saying.

"When George has these leg pains, are there any other symptoms such as fever, vomiting, or fatigue?"

"No."

"Has George been in contact with anyone who has polio?"

"I don't think so."

"Could your drinking water at the farm be infected with human waste?"

"Our outdoor toilet is about 100 feet from the well so I suppose it could be."

"So, there is a possibility that George's leg pains are the result of drinking water contaminated with the poliovirus. Someone may have used your toilet that was a carrier of the virus. Poliovirus is commonly found in sewage water, and since your outdoor toilet is close to your well, George may have acquired the virus from drinking your farm water. I am only speculating. If it is polio, we must hope that it is the non-paralytic polio, in which case he may always experience some weakness in muscles, and he may have trouble with concentration. There is nothing we can do for him at this time. So, let's just wait and see. Hopefully, he will grow out of it."

STEER AND CHICKEN
CHALLENGES

Ma and Dad's fear of polio may have contributed to the limits they placed on me socializing with friends. There were cousins my age who lived within walking distance of our farm, but I suspected that our parents conspired to keep us kids busy with farm work so we could not play together. My life was directed into farm related events, and even the one social activity to which I was entitled was farm related.

4-H was a youth organization with several clubs within each county in the state. The members in my 4-H club were farm boys and girls about my age. We met once a month in a member's home. Parents served in an advisory role. They made us stand in front of everybody and explain our choice of projects.

"George, what project would you like to work on?"

"I want to raise a steer."

"Could you tell us how you will feed and care for the steer?"

I had not thought about that, and I hated talking in front of all those people. I could never, on the spur of the moment, develop and verbalize some plan for taking care of a steer. Ma must have detected that I was tongue-tied.

"His dad and I will help him get started and guide him along."

I liked beef cattle partly because I did not have to milk them twice a day. Dad fully supported my choice of projects because he also raised Aberdeen

Angus steers. Aberdeen Angus were a black, short, blocky, and gentle breed of beef cattle. A steer was a male bull that was castrated to reduce its sexual urges and to enhance the quality of its meat. A steer's value was in its meat, so once it was up to butchering size, it was destined for the slaughterhouse.

In the spring, Dad and I visited a couple of farms that sold Aberdeen Angus calves. Farmers priced a calf according to its registered pedigree. A calf from a prized cow and bull sold for a lot of money. I had to select a calf within our price range that I thought could mature into a winner at the county fair competition in the fall.

I trained this 200-pound steer to walk beside me with a rope halter that was fastened behind its ears and around its nose. My young steer initially did not like the halter and would stubbornly plant all four legs so that he did not have to move. I tugged, yanked, and jerked on the rope, then got behind him and pushed his rear end, at which time he saw his opportunity to escape. He took off running with the rope trailing behind him. I had to capture him and start the training all over again. When I finally got him trained with the halter, I introduced him to a three-foot long wooden stick with a nail at the end to gently poke under his belly so that he kept his back level. I used that prod to poke behind his feet, so that he would position his legs square and straight under his body frame. I washed this steer, trimmed his hair, wiped his rear end, braided his tail, and painted his hooves black. After a lot of time and patience, I had a handsome and obedient steer, but he was not judged to be a first-place blue ribbon winner at the county fair.

It seemed like this kid from another 4-H club always had a better steer with good frame size, muscle development, and structure. His dad had a lot of money that he made from hauling farm animals to market in his fleet of semi-trucks. In the spring, this kid and his dad were able to drive around the country to visit farms that raised purebred Aberdeen Angus cattle and search for the best calf. They could pay any amount of money for it. This kid usually took first place at the county fair and I came in second. Second place at the county fair was still good enough for me to exhibit my steer in higher competition at the state fair.

The state fair was rife with farm kid competition and some dissension. It seemed like some boys had to prove their manliness, so they stirred up problems for meeker kids like me. I fell into their trap by impulsively saying or doing things without thinking of the repercussions. What came out of my mouth was often the result of an ill-conceived thought process that sometimes got me into trouble.

At the state fair, boys were housed overnight in a youth dormitory and we each slept in a bunkbed. Another kid got the bottom bunk, so I got the top. Some boys from another county started throwing rubber balls back and forth. One of the balls went sailing by my head. Trying to be funny, I mindlessly bellowed out: "Somebody's throwing their balls in here."

The dormitory had an adult chaperone who heard me, so he came looking for those boys. He found them and took away their balls. The next morning, when the chaperone was gone, the ball-tossing boys came looking for the guy who ratted on them which, of course, was me. They flashed a sharp razor blade.

"Whenever we find the rat, we are going to cut his nuts off."

Farm boys knew how to do a castration. It was a common farm task to castrate boar piglets, bull calves, and to even caponize rooster chickens. Castration was done to enhance the quality of the meat in farm animals. Supposedly it made a difference in flavor, texture, fat composition, and overall palatability of the meat. There were a couple of differing methods for doing castration. One was elastration which consisted of snapping a rubber band around the animal's testicle. The other option was to perform a surgical type castration, which we always did with our male pigs. The razor blades revealed that these boys were obviously looking to do a pig-type castration.

I used to help Dad castrate our animals, so I knew what it was all about. My job was to grab the baby pig and turn it upside down in my lap with its head between my legs. I had to be careful. An angry piglet could potentially bite me in a delicate area. Dad spread its rear legs, used a razor blade to cut open each testicle and cut off the pig's nuts. After Dad completed his procedure, he doused the wound with some oil and kerosene mixture to help it heal. After it was over, I gently set the pig down on some soft straw bedding material. Obviously, this procedure was stressful for the pig, but most recovered quickly.

I was terrified that these ball-throwing dormitory guys with the razor blades were not just making a threat. I was not interested in finding out if the threat was real or not, or in getting involved in a physical altercation, so I hurriedly got my pants on and rushed out of the dormitory. I never overnighted in there again, fearing that they were still looking for me. Instead I spent the remainder of my nights at the state fair sleeping in the barn on the straw, snuggled in comfort next to my Angus steer.

4-H steers were raised until their weight was optimum for slaughter. The state fair in the fall coincided with the time when they peaked in weight. 4-H kids led their steers into a show arena and paraded them in front of buyers. Buyers were most interested in steers that appeared to show the best potential for quality meat, so the best-looking steers brought the most money. The highest bidder became the new owner of the steer. It was a heartbreaking, but necessary moment for 4-H kids to separate from their beloved animal. They had learned to love their steers from the time they were a small calf in the spring to the time they were now sold to these slaughterhouse buyers in the fall. A lot of tears were shed, especially by the young girls who seemed to get emotional as they led their steers up the ramp on the back of the waiting semi-truck.

"Bye Sammy, I love you."

They knew that by the end of the day, their beloved steer would be turned into steaks and ground hamburger. Understanding the fate of farm animals was all part of growing up as a farm kid. Except for a dog and a bunch of cats, the purpose of farm animals was to provide a livelihood for our family and food for many other families.

Ma and Dad made enough money from the sale of milk, eggs, and meat to buy essentials like food and clothing, but not much else. One of Ma's projects was to raise chickens, and every day we gathered the eggs from the one hundred or so chickens housed in the chicken coop (rhymes with poop). The coop had an accumulation of chicken manure, which had a strong ammonia-like smell that burned my eyes and nostrils. As soon as I opened the door to the coop, the chickens started their obnoxious squawking, cackling, and clucking sounds. Some dumb chickens laid their eggs on the floor, so I had to be careful where I walked. Smarter chickens, if there was such a thing, went into small wooden boxes to lay their eggs. Their eggs rolled out the bottom of the box onto a sloped wooden tray. Egg gathering was easy if the eggs rolled out of the boxes as designed. Some chickens were broody, elected to sit on their egg, and would not let it roll out the box. Chickens evidently sensed that I did not like them. When I tried to reach under their belly to collect their egg, they pecked my hand with their sharp pointed beaks. I could have wrung their necks then and there, but out of consideration for Ma's hard work to raise those stupid animals, I let them survive.

Ma sold the eggs to a local egg distributor. She saved up a little extra money one year from the sale of her chicken eggs to buy a floor model black and white television. Saturday night was TV watching night after the chores were done. Ma liked to watch Lawrence Welk; Dad and I liked Eliott Ness and *The Untouchables*. We agreed to switch off so that every other Saturday night Dad and I had to watch Lawrence Welk. I kind of learned to like Myron Floren and his accordion, and the beautiful singing Lennon Sisters.

"And a-one and a-two."

The bubble machine blew bubbles as his band played *Champagne Music*. Ma and Dad even got up and danced a couple of times.

Dad liked *The Untouchables* because he could relate to that show. During prohibition, Al Capone's gangsters from Chicago frequently drove by Dad's farm to make whiskey in a nearby still. They set up the still at a farm just across the road from our farm, down a quarter-mile long obscure driveway that had been carved through an area of steep glacial deposits. Dad talked about the semi-truck loads of sugar going back there. It was well guarded by the gangsters, who posted lookouts on the bluffs. Dad liked booze so he would occasionally ask the guards for a jug of their freshly made whiskey.

The guards made it clear to Dad, "If you are ever asked, you don't know anything about where it came from. Understand?"

One day, as Dad told it, the gangsters got wind of the Feds planning to raid their bootlegging operation, so they all fled town. The Feds came in with axes and chopped holes in each of the wooden staves on the whiskey vats, rendering them unusable. They arrested the farmer who owned the property. He was the only one who went to jail for the bootlegging operation. A couple of episodes of *The Untouchables* referred to Al Capone's bootlegging operations.

EARLY EDUCATION

There were fifteen students in my one-room, rural grade school. Mrs. Militzer taught all eight grades. The schoolhouse was an old wooden building that had just enough space for a desk for the teacher and for each of the students. The student desks had bench seats, a slanted, hinged wood top that the student could lift to store books and writing materials, and an ink well in the upper right corner into which we could dip our quill pens. Eighth graders were seated in the back; first graders in the front; all others in the middle. Mrs. Militzer kept a yardstick by her desk in case there were unruly kids.

There was no indoor plumbing. We had to use an outdoor toilet at recess unless we could convince the teacher we had to go immediately. On wintry mornings, the only heat in the building radiated from a potbelly wood-fired stove. Dad stacked a supply of wood for the stove in the entryway. On nice days, we played outside during recess. A favorite sport was *Annie Annie over*. Teams for each side were chosen by the two eighth graders. I hated to get chosen last. One team stood on one side of the school and the other team on the other side. The team with the ball threw it over the roof of the school to the other side. Members of the team on the other side would scramble to catch the ball as it bounced off the roof. If they caught it, they could sneak around the building and tag a player on the other side who would then be out of the game. If they failed to catch it, they threw it back and hollered, "Annie, Annie, over."

27

When I was in sixth grade, that school was closed and all the students were consolidated with several other one-room school students in the area into a larger grade school in town. A new high school was built for grades nine through twelve, so local students would not have to be bused to a distant town for high school. My class was the first to start in this new high school as freshmen. Sophomores, juniors, and seniors who lived in the area and who attended high school elsewhere were transferred to the new school. There was definitely a pecking order, with seniors at the top.

The school had very few boys, and even fewer boys who were athletic, so any boy who wanted to play basketball made the varsity team. I thought sports would be exciting and would maybe give me some notoriety, so I joined the team and found myself playing on a varsity team with upperclassmen. I did not know how to play basketball. I had never even held a basketball in my hands until I started seventh grade. I could not dribble without looking down at the ball, my shots were terrible except for lay ups, and I was an all-around bad player. For some ridiculous reason, the coach saw something in me that made him think that I could play basketball.

"George, I am going to have you start on the varsity team. You will play point guard and direct the plays for the offense."

I was both delighted and fearful. Here I was, an incompetent, socially awkward freshman who was out of his element but was now a starting guard on the varsity basketball team playing with these older boys. One night after a game, a couple of them decided to get revenge. On the bus home, they approached me like they were befriending me.

"Would you like some of our pop?"

Ma and Dad never had soda in the house, so I thought that it would be a real treat. I took a swig, spit it out, and started to gag. They had peed in the bottle. They all laughed. I was dejected and nearly in tears as I slumped into my seat on the bus. The basketball coach later recognized that I was not a good basketball player and thankfully relegated me to second string.

That singular event etched a compulsive, obsessive, almost frantic need in my mind to get revenge in my own way for the conduct of those bullies. I wanted to be better than them. I wanted to achieve such lofty goals and recognition in my life that they would feel shame for having done this to me. It was one of the first negative motivators that drove me to strive for a great destiny.

DRINKING AND DRIVING

By the time I was a junior in high school, my social status started to change. Basketball, football, and baseball were the only sports in my school, and I played all three. Football was based on eight-man teams because there were not enough boys for an eleven-man team. Most players smoked, so we were usually out of breath after the first few plays of the game. If the team won one game each season, it was cause for a celebration. I did not play sports to win; I played to get attention.

I was lucky to latch onto a steady girlfriend during my junior and senior years. She was tall, slender, charming, and cordial, and I saw her as beautiful in every way. Her name was Pat and she was in a class behind me. She also happened to be our minister's daughter. I never figured out what she saw in me, but I mentally speculated that the other good-looking girls in school had already hooked up with all the popular jocks and I was all that was left. I wanted to see her often, so I went to her dad's church on a regular basis. It was the church on the hill that was visible from Dad's farm. She lived in the parsonage next to the church. I knew she would be at church every Sunday, so I volunteered to be the head usher so that I could sit in the back pew. During her dad's long monotonous sermons, I sometimes fell asleep thinking that it would not be noticed from his pulpit in front of the church. He probably saw my head bobbing.

At age seventeen, I was into weekend partying and drinking—mostly beer but sometimes even hard liquor. It was easy to get booze in my town. With a population of only five hundred people, the town had six taverns, whose owners all wanted to make money. Age was not a factor in determining who they sold liquor to. My drinking routine was to buy a case of beer and drink it while driving around on the back-country roads. One road was a dead end in an obscure location with a long farm driveway at the end, so it became a favorite parking spot to have a party. A bigger town nearby had beer bars for eighteen-year-olds. It was not hard to get into them at age sixteen or seventeen by crowding the bouncers policing the entrance. Occasionally, one of us would get stopped, then we would try again when the next crowd surged at the door. On the trip home from the bars, I drag-raced my cousin John, who was a neighbor and a friend. Dad's new '61 Chevy Impala six-cylinder would get up to ninety mph. It was frustrating that I could not get more speed out of it in order to beat John's older '55 eight-cylinder 265 horsepower Chevy Bel Air.

The drinking lifestyle was prevalent among the youth—as well as adults—around town, but it was not without consequences. A couple of intoxicated upperclassmen were driving out of town at a high rate of speed and failed to negotiate a curve. Their car rolled several times. Talk of the town was that their bodies were so badly mangled that the undertaker could not show them in the casket. About a half mile further down that same road, the mother of one of my classmates was T-boned by a drunk driver who failed to stop at a stop sign. A little further past our farm, there was another fatality when a drunk drifted off the road into the ditch and rolled several times. Late one evening, a canning factory truck driver was hauling wash water from the peas to dump on a farm field across the road from our farm. A young boy was sitting on the back of the flat-bed truck beside a half-full 500-gallon tank of the wash water. The driver had been drinking, failed to realize the danger of the shifting weight of water in the tank, and tried to speed around the corner. The water sloshed to one side, the truck rolled, and the boy was crushed by the tank. These fatalities all occurred within one mile of Dad's farm, and all were the consequence of drunk driving. That section of highway should have been nicknamed *highway from hell.*

During the summer before my senior year, Pat developed a friendship with a lady who came to town to work in the canning factory. She was in her early thirties and seemed to take an interest in me as a good friend. She was quiet, soft spoken, and strikingly beautiful, with big blue eyes. I enjoyed staring at beautiful ladies, and I think she enjoyed the attention. It was outwardly obvious that she was having difficulties in her life. When she looked at me, her sad eyes pierced the innermost chambers of my heart, sort of like cupid's arrow. In my typically uncouth manner, I asked her what was going on in her life. There was no verbal response, just big tears streaming down her puffy red cheeks. I felt like a piece of crap for asking the question.

She met this forty-something-year-old guy at the canning factory who evidently schmoozed her into thinking that he was the answer to all her problems. For some ungodly reason, she appeared to be attracted to this lecherous coot. He seemed to want more from her than he deserved. I tried to accept her judgment about him, so Pat and I agreed to go along with them for a night of drinking and driving. I mostly went along to check the guy out.

We were riding in his beat-up old Studebaker on the road to Pat's house. The road had sharp, winding curves leading up to the church and the parsonage at the top of the hill. Approaching one of the curves, I had the urge to open my big mouth and brag.

"I can take that curve at forty miles per hour."

He responded, "That's nothing. Watch this."

Soon we were going eighty, heading into the curve with the tires squealing, and all of us getting tossed around in the car. The car was nearly sideways in the road. We made it, but I could not wait to get back home and get out of that car. He may have sensed that I was less than happy with his foolish stunt as I quickly exited the car and slammed the door behind me. Shortly after that, to my delight, and possibly after my gentle persuasion, Pat's friend informed him that she was discontinuing their friendship. She said that he looked heartbroken and distraught.

Shortly after our friend terminated her relationship with that guy, I was walking down our driveway to get the mail. Dad's farm driveway exited off County Road G. It was the same driveway on which I did my tractor spin-around stunt. A ditch running parallel to the road was about five feet deep, with some rather steep embankments. There were no guardrails, so if a driver wandered off the road into the ditch, he was not going to get back onto the road. A gravel-covered steel culvert was installed into the ditch so we could cross over it into our farm driveway.

I was alarmed by a car driving down the ditch at a high rate of speed. I recognized the car; it was the same Studebaker in which we had gone around that curve at eighty mph. It appeared to be aiming directly at me and was not slowing down. I ran to get out of the way. Perhaps the driver was holding me responsible for his breakup with our friend. The car continued full speed down the ditch, hit the culvert head on, flipped upside down, and went airborne across the driveway. The sound of bending metal and crashing glass was loud. It landed on its roof in the ditch on the other side of the culvert. Fire started flaring up under the crumpled hood. I ran to the overturned car, looked inside and it was a horrible scene. Blood was splattered all over the front seat. The driver's body was limp, and he was bleeding profusely from his mouth and nose. His head was bobbing up and down. I reached through a busted window to try and hold his head steady, thinking it would help, but soon realized it was not doing any good.

I knew that crashed cars sometimes exploded, so I ran back to the shed to get the Farmall C tractor and a logging chain so that I could upright the car and pull him out. I raced back to the car. I drove crossways down through the ditch trying to figure out where to hook the chain on his car. About that same time, Ma and Dad saw what was happening and called Doctor Sharp, the local volunteer fire department, and the police. They showed up within a short time and took over extricating the guy's contorted body from the twisted smoldering wreckage. I stood back and watched. In the newspaper the next day, there was an article that the guy died on the way to the hospital.

There were still pigs to slop, eggs to gather, and cows in the barn that needed to be milked that night. I cranked up the radio in the barn tuned to WLS in Chicago and tried to focus on the top hits from the '50s. Nobody in my family talked about tragic events like this, so my mind was enveloped into a deep thought process. What if? What if that fellow was already suicidal when Pat and I were in the car with him going around that curve at eighty mph? What kept that car upright and on the road that night? It most certainly should have rolled multiple times, but why didn't it? Maybe someday I will know the answer.

TURNING POINT

By my senior year, I considered high school to be a waste of time. I gave up on any attempt to be studious because I was destined to be a farmer so why should I put out any extra effort for good grades? My grades were mediocre at best with a C average. I had established a somewhat comfortable rapport with my English teacher. I liked her and tried to be nice to her because she was young, petite, and attractive, with a pleasant demeanor.

I recklessly put my relationship with her to a test. There was a writing assignment due in her class. Thinking she was a pushover, a couple of us guys decided to copy the paper of one of our girl classmates. We made some minor alterations and then submitted it as our own. After the teacher read it, it was obvious to her that we were cheating. She could not let it pass without taking some action, so she sent a letter to our parents stating that she was going to flunk us. It meant we would not graduate from high school on time. More time in school meant more time away from our farm duties, so our dads got involved. They scheduled a meeting with the teacher that resulted in a compromise. She needed to provide us a private class to get us to a level where we could pass the course and still graduate from high school on schedule.

I loved the private class and the teacher was amazingly still nice to us. She required us to write a paper on a subject of our choice, and this time it better be our own work. I decided to write about the investigation of aircraft accidents. It was a far cry from anything to do with farming, but there must have been another reason why I chose it.

Perhaps it was the B-58 Hustler flights over the farm, or I may have picked up an inspiration toward aviation from a close acquaintance of Dad's. He was the brother of Dad's first wife. Something happened in the early years of his home life that forced him to live away from home. Dad offered him room and board in exchange for work at the farm so he could get his life in order. After he left Dad's farm, he somehow got involved in developing and manufacturing a system to supply oxygen to aircrew during flight in the WWII time frame. His business name was Zepp Aero and he located it near a large aircraft manufacturing facility in California. His success was evidenced by pictures of his home in Beverly Hills next to some of the movie stars.

He never forgot the kind deeds that Dad did for him so every year when he returned to visit family, he always stopped at Dad's farm. He was a tall fellow with a fat face and beaming eyes. When he talked to you, he kind of looked down at you but did so in a respectful manner. He was a pilot and owned his own airplane. He noticed that I was enamored by his stories, so he directed his flying-related conversations toward me.

For my English paper on the investigation of aircraft accidents, I started gathering information in my small high school library. I found the address for an Air Force base in the big city about fifty miles away and sent a letter addressed to *Anybody* requesting information about aircraft accident investigation. It landed on the desk of the Air Force flight safety officer at the base, who was also a fighter pilot. He sent me an immediate response.

> *Dear George,*
>
> *Your letter requesting information about the investigation of aircraft accidents was forwarded to me. I would be pleased to talk to you about this subject. I see that your address is a rural address. I can drive to your farm, pick you up, and bring you back to the base. We will tour the fighter jets on*

the flight line, and I will show you my office, where I have considerable information about the investigation of aircraft accidents. Please let me know when you would like to visit the base.

> *Sincerely,*
> *Herb Ritke*
> *Captain, US Air Force*

I was excited, so I immediately responded with a suggested date for Captain Ritke to pick me up. He showed me around the air base and let me sit in an F-102 fighter jet airplane. We went to the Air Force club for dinner, where he bought me several hard liquor drinks that tasted great. I had a tolerance for drinking beer but not for drinking hard liquor. He took me to his home for the evening where I exhibited my deficiency in social graces by puking in his toilet. The next morning, I recovered from my drunkenness, and he took me back to the farm.

The information I learned from my experience at the Air Force base inspired me to write a great paper for the class. The teacher was pleased, Dad was pleased—everybody was happy.

Capt. Ritke was the father of two young boys whom he wanted to expose to a farm environment. I was happy to reciprocate his kindness to me by showing his boys around the farm. I drove the young boys out to our fields and down through the woods on the tractor, showed them the cows in the barn, and let them pet the cats and dog. I tried to make it into a fun event by demonstrating how I could hypnotize a chicken. I had done this before so I knew it would work. I snatched one of Ma's chickens by the leg, tipped it on its side, and gently laid its head down against the ground. I waved my free hand across its head and in a deep, slow voice said, "Abracadabra, alakazam."

I raised my hands off the chicken, and it remained motionless in place. "Voila! See, I just hypnotized a chicken."

The kids were fascinated, and I loved the chance to show off one of my few farm kid skills. Eventually, the chicken got up and ran away.

In the summer of 1962, an event occurred at the farm that would be forever cemented in my mind. I was combining grain in a back field (the *com* is emphasized). Our combine was a 1950s-era gas engine powered harvester that was pulled by our powerful seventy-horsepower John Deere G tractor. The engine on the combine was about the same size as the tractor engine and made about the same amount of noise. It powered a sickle bar, canvas apron, beater bars, and the shaker mechanism. All together the components in the combine cut the oats, thrashed the grain seeds from the stems, and conveyed the grain into a hopper. The clunking, swishing, and clanging of those combine components plus the roar of the engines on both the combine and the tractor made so much noise that if you were trying to talk to someone in the vicinity, you needed to shout to be heard.

I was driving the tractor when I was startled by a deafening roar that thundered from the sky and drowned out all other noises. The ground was trembling. I looked up to the sky. A fighter jet was flying so low over the farm that it appeared to be on a flight path to crash in our field. A long stream of fire spewed from the rear of the aircraft. Then, like a bolt of lightning streaking across the sky, it quickly disappeared into the distance. I sat there in awe at what I had just seen, hoping that it would return, but it was gone. I suspected that the pilot flying that jet had to be the fighter pilot who befriended me for information about my English paper. Who else would know the location of our farm and fly directly over it at tree top level and lightning fast speeds? He later wrote to confirm that it was him. After that, my thinking was focused on one dream in life. It would satisfy my need for adventure, thrill, risk, and notoriety. I had to fly fighter jets.

Captain Ritke advised me on the many things I had to think about if I wanted to fly fighter jets in the Air Force. There were requirements to get a college degree, get a commission as an officer, and be in good health. Getting into college was probably a long shot because of my screw-off attitude in high school. Even if I did get into college, Air Force officer candidates needed to demonstrate strong leadership qualities before being considered for a commission and I possessed few of those attributes. I was good at hard manual labor, but most of the leadership traits that I acquired were from bossing cows and pigs around, if that counted for anything.

Farm accidents had left visible, puffy scarring on my hand and leg. Childhood illnesses resulted in weakness in my legs. A painfully chronic whiplash injury that I sustained from a car accident never fully healed. If I could somehow overcome these hurdles, then I needed to get through an intensive Air Force pilot training program before flying fighter jets. These obstacles seemed insurmountable. For now, it seemed best if I just stayed focused on farming.

Two years of farming after high school gave me a lot of time to think about whether I wanted to pursue a long-shot dream or continue to work on a farm that was devoid of glamour, was physically hard, and offered few satisfactions for my adventurous desires.

The farm had beef cattle, pigs, chickens, ducks, and dairy cows, all of which needed lots of care. Cows needed to be milked twice a day, 365 days a year, unless they were dried up during the summer months so their bodies could work to produce a calf. Not all the cows were bred to produce calves because Dad still needed income from the sale of milk, so there were always cows to be milked. There were no vacations, and no days off.

Temporary help to take over the cow duties for a day was not possible because cows were accustomed to seeing only Dad, Ma, or me. If a stranger walked into the barn, the cows got antsy. Any unusual disturbance seemed to cause a cow to jump around, switch its tail, kick, buck, crap, and urinate. Maybe it was my imagination, but cows seemed to develop an attitude to suit their mood. I detected a smirk on their face when they used their tail to swat me across my face with the urine of an adjacent cow. It seemed like they sometimes did it on purpose, and one time it got on my nerves. I twisted that cow's tail to get it to stop and the cow responded by giving me a swift kick to my face. She broke off my front tooth. I had to go to the dentist, whose appropriate name was Dr Moen, to get the roots of the tooth removed. Dad had a lot of respect and love for his animals but if an animal misbehaved, it was off to the slaughterhouse, and, in this case, to get money to pay for my dental bill. It was one less cow I had to milk.

Cows not only ate a lot, they crapped a lot. A chain driven barn-cleaner moved manure down the gutters, outside the barn and into a manure spreader. The manure spreader was used to spread the manure onto the fields, which was not my favorite job. A chain on the bottom of the spreader box conveyed the manure into two rotating beater bars attached to the rear of the spreader. They had several small spokes on them that flung the manure across the field. On cold, wintry days, the chain on the manure spreader would freeze up so I had to try to get it free by digging through the manure with my hands to loosen it with a prybar. The manure contained a lot of liquid from cow urine. On windy days, I quickly learned to determine wind direction before flinging manure in the field.

Several acres of crops were grown in the farm fields for animal feed. Dad had maintained the soil in those fields in fertile condition. He fed the soil with an application of rich cow manure in the winter, and the soil responded in the summer and fall by providing bountiful harvests of corn, oats, and alfalfa. Spring, summer, and fall fieldwork consisted of planting, weeding, and harvesting crops. Alfalfa was cut, baled, and manually stacked in the barn's haymow; corn stalks were chopped for sileage and blown into the silo.

Some corn was left on the stalk to mature, and the ears were stripped from the stalks with a powered machine. The corn picker was connected to the tractor via a shaft that was geared into two rollers on the picker that were spaced about two inches apart. Those large solid-iron rollers measured about six inches in diameter, were five feet long, and had several dull protrusions running their full length which enabled the rollers to strip the ears of corn from their stalks. The rollers spun at a high rate of speed.

The corn stalks were fed into these fast spinning rollers as the picker was pulled forward by the tractor. After ears of corn were stripped from the stalk, they were conveyed into a wagon that was pulled behind the corn picker. The harvested corn was stored in a corn crib and used as feed for the animals in the winter.

This corn picker would have made a good medieval torture machine. It was fraught with human hazard, especially when the farmer did not respect the power and speed of those rollers. Not all the corn in the field grew perfectly vertical. Some were tipped to the side due to winds, or the weight of the ear of corn on the stalk. These crooked stalks frequently bunched up in front of the rollers and prevented more corn stalks from going through the rollers. The farmer had to stop, get off the tractor, and try to pull the jammed corn stalks out of the rollers. For the sake of expediency, some farmers did this without first stopping the machine. As the farmer pulled on the stalk, the spinning rollers suddenly grabbed onto it and pulled it through the rollers. It all happened so fast that if the farmer was still hanging on, his arm got pulled between the fast spinning rollers. Both the corn stalk and his arm got shredded.

Like many farmers, I was carelessly comfortable around farm equipment and sometimes oblivious to its danger. One fall day, I was picking corn when, predictably, a bunch of corn stalks got lodged in front of the two rollers. I got off the tractor and yanked a couple of the stalks out of the jammed-up bunch. As I was reaching to grab for another handful, the spinning rollers suddenly latched onto them and rapidly zipped them through the machine. I looked at my two arms to confirm that they were still intact. It got me thinking that with my frame of mind about danger, farming could be detrimental to my long-term survival.

Growing productive crops on the fields required time-consuming attention to controlling weeds. Cultivating weeds out of the corn began in the spring as soon as the planted corn seeds germinated and revealed the corn rows in the field. I attached a cultivator to our mid-size John Deere B tractor. The digging component of the cultivator consisted of small shovels on the end of solid iron shanks, which stirred up the soil and upended the weeds as the tractor pulled it forward. Cultivating corn required constant attention to precise tractor guidance so that the cultivator did not dig out corn instead of weeds. It was a slow and boring task. Constant attention to cultivating did not mean that my mind could not wander.

Oats and alfalfa were not suitable for mechanical cultivation because they were densely seeded and therefore did not have row spacing that could be cultivated. Weeds still poked their heads out from above the crop. One nasty persistent weed was the Canadian thistle that had sharp needle-like prickles on its leaves. Feathery wind-blown seeds from the thistle heads could reseed themselves throughout the farm causing thousands, and maybe even millions more thistles in the fields the next year. I had to wear gloves and a long sleeve shirt on hot summer days as I walked through the oats and alfalfa fields with a sheep shear in my hand to clip the heads off these thistles. I carefully stuffed them into a paper bag and burned them.

Quack grass could smother any crop because of its dense underground root system. It rapidly propagated from the rhizomes of its roots. A small patch of quack grass one year could easily turn into a large patch the next year. Dad was insistent on controlling it. We dug quack grass with a pitchfork; shook the dirt off the roots; piled the roots together and burned them. Weeding was a time-consuming summer task on the farm.

Dad was working me into the entire farm routine. He was in his sixties and spending more time at his favorite hangouts in town, and justifiably so. He had worked hard to support his family. His absence meant that I needed to complete my farm duties before I could go out at night and party. Farm chores were always a priority. As I was beginning to see it, hard work with no days off would continue for the rest of my life if I remained a farmer.

GOTTA DO IT

As I worked on these mundane farm tasks, my wandering mind was focused on the hurdles that I needed to surpass to reach my deep-seated desire to become a fighter pilot.

How can I get a college degree? Do I have the capabilities to get a commission as an officer in the US Air Force? Can I maintain 20/20 vision and pass an Air Force flight physical? Do I have what it takes to get through pilot training to fly fighter jets?

I started to gather information, but it was very explorative. I did it secretly, so Ma and Dad did not find out. I mailed a letter to the University of Wisconsin to inquire about admission requirements. Algebra and trigonometry were required prior to even being considered for admission. Since I was not studious in high school, I did not have those courses. My small high school did not even offer trigonometry. How could I complete those courses? I learned that the university extension offered them by correspondence.

Overhead lighting in my bedroom in the old farmhouse was less than ideal for studying so I bought a floor lamp to preserve my 20/20 eyesight. I had been involved in a car accident a couple of years prior in which I was rear ended by a drunk driver on the way home from a modified car race. To study without neck pain, I made a wood rack to position the books directly in front of me at eye level while I wore a plastic neck brace to hold my head up. I also drank a little brandy to ease the pain. Dad used to hide his brandy bottles from Ma, so I tried to do the same. I knew most of his hiding spots. One was in the locked toolbox in the shed, but I knew where the key was hidden, so I sneaked an occasional swig from his bottle. Ma found the bottle I hid in my room while she was gathering up my dirty clothes and she shamed me into stopping.

Every day, I watched for the mailman and ran to beat Ma to the mailbox to get the next correspondence lesson. I worked on the algebra lessons after my chores were finished, then hid the books from Ma, although she probably suspected I was up to something. It was exciting to think that I was taking the first step toward reaching my goal of becoming a fighter pilot. Algebra was easy for me and I got a good grade in the course. I was always good with numbers and liked math. I looked forward to trigonometry which was a little more challenging. I quickly finished trig, got a good grade, and immediately applied for admission to the university. It was all sort of a trial that maybe would not go very far, but it was fun to see how far I could go with it. The university acceptance policy was to grant admission to all qualified in-state applicants. High school grades were considered for admission but were only disqualifying if I had failed any course. Luckily, my high school English teacher had given me a passing grade for writing a good paper, so I was okay on the failure part.

I was getting increasingly burned out on farm life. Milking cows twice a day without ever getting a day off, the hard labor in the fields, the risks with little reward, and the lack of an adventurous and glamourous lifestyle all played a role in my thinking. I wanted thrills and maybe even a little notoriety, so I was ready to move on to a new challenge in life. I had to overcome one big hurdle before going any further in this process and it would be a tough one: I had to tell Ma and Dad that I was leaving the farm. I had to do it soon because school was starting in a month.

At the kitchen table one night during supper, I finally got enough courage to tell them I was going to college. It was the 1960s, and the Vietnam War was starting to heat up, so I did not want to alarm Ma with any mention about being a military fighter pilot. I knew Dad's heart was set on me taking over the farm. At sixty-two years of age, he would be stuck with doing all the farm work himself. Dad's reaction was less than enthusiastic, but he seemed to understand that he had to let me go off on my own for a while to get this university stuff out of my system. After all, he once did a similar thing to his dad when he went off and drove a fuel truck for a couple of years while his dad continued to operate the farm. Dad eventually returned to take over the family farm. Dad was probably thinking that I would come back to the farm after my first year of college, if not sooner, and then stay put.

PART TWO

YOU'LL NEVER MAKE IT

Incoming students at the University of Wisconsin in Madison were required to meet with an academic advisor prior to signing up for classes. My meeting did not go well. It quickly devolved into another introduction to the realm of negative motivation. He looked at my high school grades, shook his head, and said, "George, you will never make it at this university."

It was obvious that I did not have the prerequisites to enroll in my first choice of studies. Mechanical engineering students were proficient in using a slide rule; I had never heard of a slide rule. The advisor told me I did not have the prerequisites to enroll at the university in mechanical engineering, or for that matter, in any program except possibly letters and science. He strongly encouraged me to first enroll in a local technical school and take elementary courses that would prepare me for college. I saw that as a problem because the Air Force had an age limit for entering pilot training. If I had to go to a technical school first, most of the course credits would not count toward getting a degree from the university. I would be too old when I eventually graduated from college to enter pilot training. I mumbled something about giving up on my Dad's farm to pursue a dream of becoming a fighter pilot. Evidently the advisor sensed a strong determination, and he gave me the okay to enroll in the university with the provision that he could dictate my first semester courses. Except for one, they were not fun courses.

I had not previously thought about it, but I needed a place to live. The university housing office had a list of names and addresses of places to rent. Many rooms were already booked for the upcoming semester, so my options were limited. There was a dumpy old residential house in my price range that was within walking distance of all university buildings. A rich dentist owned it and used its prime location to his advantage by cramming as many students into it as possible. It had several walled off rooms in both the upper and lower levels. The room that was still available was a shared upstairs bedroom with a bunk bed. I was the second person to rent the room, so I got the top bunk.

The learning process at this university was quite impersonal; some lecture class sizes were larger than the entire population of my hometown. Teaching assistants were available to answer questions during smaller discussion sessions, but I was uncomfortable with asking questions, even among only thirty other students. I found out how challenging college was going to be when I got the results of my first geography test. It was a pop quiz and students were given a map of the United States with a blank outline of all the states. We were supposed to label each of the states. The quiz caught me completely by surprise, so I flunked it.

The grades that I received from then on were not good, but they were not unacceptably bad. Most professors graded on a curve, which was to my advantage since some students did not seem to be sincere about getting a college education. They skewed the curve in my favor by populating the lower end of the grading curve. I only needed a "C" average to graduate from college and I could not fail any courses.

College algebra was fun, but English, history, Spanish, and geography were a real chore (it euphemistically rhymes with bore). The courses were not overly difficult for an average student, but since I had never studied in high school, I did not know how to study. I spent a lot of time taking notes, recopying articles from the library, memorizing Spanish words, and trying to figure out what was important so I could pass the endless tests. I had never heard the word *grammar* until I got to college, so English grammar was especially difficult because I did not know how to write intelligently.

The quality of my book report about *Moby Dick* reflected my feelings on the subject matter. Some of my sentences ended in a preposition, adjectives were misplaced, paragraphs started with something other than a theme sentence, train of thought was non-existent, conjunctions were wrong, and there were dangling participles, whatever all that meant. In general, my grammar was a mess and the teacher marked all the errors on my papers in red ink. I tried to hide my returned papers from the view of other students in the class. The English teacher probably gave me Cs out of the kindness of her heart because she sensed that I had a strong determination to pass her course.

The ancient history course was an eye-opening experience for me since I had been brought up to believe in God. The professor had *firm evidence* that religion was made up by men during the Neolithic period at about the same time as written word came into existence. Those biblical writers were supposedly anxious about dying so they concocted a God and an afterlife. He expected students to remember his teachings to pass the course. His evidence was not complimentary toward any religion, which included my religion of Christianity. Students in his class were tested on their retention of his supposedly vast array of knowledge and research. He seemed to relish his status as a professor to influence a captive audience of young and vulnerable minds. I hated the course because this holier-than-thou professor corrupted my gullible mind with doubts about Christianity.

I needed a break from the stress of studying, so one Friday night my roommate and I invited another fellow who lived in our house to come over for beer and some academic discussion. This guy was super intelligent. He got As in all his courses, one of which was organic chemistry that was way above my level of understanding. He had an academic scholarship into the pre-med program. His mind seemed to be like a sponge that soaked up and retained information. It made me jealous that he never had to study. My roommate was a Christian and was taking the same ancient history course as me, so our conversation with this super smart guy turned to a discussion about God.

"This history professor is teaching us that there is no God. What do you think?"

"He is right."

"What? How can that be? The Bible has many stories about the existence of God."

"What stories are those?"

I got the feeling that he was sort of playing along with me. In the end, he would zap me with some uncontestable comment.

"There is the story of God directing Noah to build an ark and to load up one species of every kind of animal before he destroyed mankind by flooding the earth."

"So how does that prove there is a God? Floods happen all the time. There is scientific evidence that the flooding referred to in the Bible only occurred in an area around the Black Sea. A comet crashed into the ocean and caused massive flooding, not the rain. Do you really think that two of each species of animals on earth would fit into one man-made boat, or that high elevations such as mountain peaks would be covered with water after only forty days of rain? There is no evidence to prove that the entire earth was flooded."

This sounded believable, so I did not have any response to counter him. My roommate had the same views on religion as me, so he chimed in with a Bible story from his childhood.

"Moses was leading the Israelites out of Egypt, and they were trying to get across the Red Sea? God parted the Red Sea, so Moses and his people were able to escape from the pursuing Egyptian troops. When they got across, the sea closed and drowned the pursuing Egyptian troops. That is a miracle that could only happen with the help of God."

"I am familiar with that story, but I doubt that it was a god who parted the sea. Natural phenomena could have caused the sea to separate. Maybe there was a wind set-down effect."

"A what?"

"When you were younger, did they not teach you about wind set-down effect in your god-training? A strong wind blowing for several hours can cause the sea level to drop."

So much for that story. After a brief thought-provoking pause, I remembered another Bible story.

"How about Daniel, who was thrown into the lion's den but was not eaten by the lions? Surely it was the work of God to save him."

"Maybe the lions weren't hungry. Animals only kill when they are hungry. These are all stories that are explainable by what we now know from science. George, have you read the entire Bible?

I had to admit that I had not.

"I have, and there is nothing in it that convinces me of the existence of a god. Just look at the idea that a god created the first two humans called Adam and Eve. Obviously, the theory of evolution has pretty much debunked that idea."

I had been indoctrinated into religion with a bias toward God. When I read the required readings from the Bible, I did not comprehend most of what I read, so I was inept at debating the true meaning behind the stories in the Bible. Ma and Dad made me attend Sunday school every week except during the summer months, when I had to go to Catechism class in preparation for confirmation. Sunday school was interesting because I learned about all the common Bible stories such as Adam and Eve, Noah, Abraham, Lot, David and Goliath, and of course, Jesus. Catechism class was taught by our much-too-holy preacher and it was painfully boring. He made me memorize not only the Ten Commandments but Luther's interpretation of what they meant. The Lord's Prayer was easy because I said it many times, but the petitions were purely rote memory. There were memory items pertaining to baptism, the sacrament of the altar, and the office of the keys and confession, plus more. To be certain that I memorized all this, there was a threat hanging over my head that I would be tested on it one Sunday in front of the entire congregation. The board of elders would decide if I passed or failed. I had to pass to get confirmed. That intense indoctrination into religion should have prepared me to defend the Bible, but the true meaning of what I learned was not comprehendible by my thirteen-year-old mind.

I never met an agnostic in my small hometown, so there were no debates about the veracity of the Bible. It was just accepted by everybody as the gospel truth. Some locals from my hometown went to church on a regular basis, but many did not. Even so, nobody ever openly disavowed the existence of God.

"Do you really believe that these Bible stories are not true?" I asked.

"I will tell you what I think. A bunch of camel-jockey ragheads with vivid imaginations sat in the middle of the desert with their legs crossed using their newfound ability to write, so they wrote a Bible. Religion, and this *God* thing were invented by man," he replied.

"Wow. That is hard to believe."

I had no recourse other than to let our discussion end on that disturbing note.

It made me wonder why, if there truly is a God, would He let a transformation away from religion happen to me? Would He not want to keep me in his flock of believers and direct my life accordingly? Even with those startling revelations from that professor and that super smart guy, I never gave up on praying at bedtime. It was part of my normal routine.

Now I lay me down to sleep, I pray the Lord my soul to keep, if I should die before I wake, I pray the Lord my soul to take.

Then I prayed the Lord's prayer,

Our father who art in heaven, hallowed be thy name. Thy kingdom come. Thy will be done, on earth as it is in heaven. Give us this day our daily bread. And forgive us our trespasses, as we forgive those who trespass against us. And lead us not into temptation, but deliver us from evil: for thine is the kingdom, and the power, and the glory forever and ever. Amen

As insurance for help in getting me through college, I threw in another sort of prayer. I did not know how to make up divine-sounding prayers since they did not teach that in catechism class. Anyway, I figured it did not matter what you said; if there was a God, He would figure out what you wanted. So, as an add-on, I asked that the Lord help me get through college and become a fighter pilot. Even if there was no God, it would not be bad to pretend like there was one.

It would be helpful if you could send me something to show that you really do exist.

And did He ever come through for me.

English class once again nearly put an end to my career ambitions. A paper was due at the end of the semester. The subject of the paper was discretionary so I could write about anything I was familiar with, even something I enjoyed writing about like flying or growing up on a farm. I started to develop it well ahead of the due date. I wrote a rough draft and put it aside for a few days, went back to it, made changes, and did this again and again over the course of several days. I asked a friend who was majoring in English to look at the paper and to suggest improvements. Most of my friend's suggestions were minor grammatical changes such as changing a few sentence structures or adding some punctuation. When I submitted it, I expected the English teacher to really like it. She might even be proud of herself for bringing me this far along in English. I was wrong.

She evaluated the paper as being *too good* to be my work and accused me of cheating. She gave me an F on the paper, which most likely meant that I would get a D or an F for the course. I was heartbroken because I had been truly inspired to write an outstanding paper. I gathered up all my hand-written rough drafts and took them to the Dean's office to try and get a reversal of her grade. After all, what did I have to lose? It did not take long to figure out that there was no way the Dean was going to overrule a teaching assistant in favor of a lowly freshman student. He and the teacher did agree to throw out the grade for that paper. My final grade for that course was based on all my coursework prior to that paper so I got a C for the course.

My grades for the first semester for all the courses resulted in a 2.2 grade point average based on a 4.0 scale. All I needed was seven more semesters of 2.0 or better to get a college degree; I did not need any stellar academic performance.

ROTC

Every able-bodied male freshman at the university was required to attend an orientation about the military programs that were offered on campus. The university publicized that they took attendance. Many guys tried to avoid it because they detested the military. If a student's name did not show up on the attendance roster, it was unlikely there were any repercussions. Knowing that a commission was required to get into pilot training, I attended.

Reserve Officer Training Corp or ROTC was one avenue for getting a commission as an officer in the military. Officer Training School (OTS) was another avenue. A third route was the Air Force Academy, but it was off-limits for me because of my mediocre grades in high school. ROTC was a four-year university program that required attendance at a class every week. Upon successful completion of the program, a cadet would be awarded a commission as a second lieutenant in the US Air Force.

I knew absolutely nothing about ROTC and little about OTS until attending this mandatory orientation. I just knew that I needed a commission to get into pilot training. The briefing also described OTS, which involved getting a college degree first, then enlisting in the Air Force as an airman, then applying for OTS training to get a commission. With OTS, I risked getting stuck in the Air Force as an enlisted airman, never getting a commission, and never making it to pilot training. OTS sounded like it was sort of a crap shoot, whereas ROTC sounded good. At least with

ROTC, when I graduated from college, I would be almost guaranteed to get a commission, assuming there were no glitches. I signed up for ROTC.

Attendance at both an academic class and a military drill period was required. The academic class emphasized military history and leadership. Cadets were required to study and take tests just like any other academic course at the university. The class counted for one credit, which was applied toward the 120 credits needed to graduate. The freshman ROTC course was easy; but, for one credit, I would not have expected it to be very difficult.

During one of my first ROTC classes, the instructor informed the class that in our sophomore year we would be required to stand in front of the class to give a speech and to pass a five-hour long Air Force Officer Qualification written test (AFOQT). The test measured verbal and math aptitude. For pilot candidates, there were additional tests to determine aviation aptitude.

The speech was intended to be an evaluation of an ROTC cadet's ability to develop a professional presentation and to effectively communicate in front of an audience. As a farm kid, I had never done any public speaking and was scared to death of speaking in front of any audience. Now, I would have to do a speech in front of all these other cadets. I worried that I would clam up, freeze, stutter, forget everything, pass out, sweat, or puke—or all of those. The thought of having to do public speaking probably caused an increase in my already unsightly acne, stiffness in my neck, loss of appetite, and whatever else could make the situation worse. I had a year to worry about it.

I was issued an Air Force blue uniform consisting of shirt, pants, hat, socks, and shoes and was required to attend a mandatory once-a-week drill session. Upperclassmen inspected my uniform, shoeshine, and haircut. I had to learn military drill commands and march in formation.

"Forward, march."

"Hut two three four, hut two three four."

"Get in step, Cadet Kohn. What is your problem? Do you have your shoes on the wrong feet? Next time, I better see a spit shine on those shoes."

I had to spend considerable time at home applying several coats of black shoe polish, letting it dry, and then spitting on it as I rubbed it with a soft cloth. I tried to get the glossy appearance that they demanded.

Humiliation was part of the process.

"Cadet Kohn, your gig line is atrocious. When you show up here next week, it better be straight."

Gig line referred to the seam on the shirt, the belt buckle, and the zipper on the pants. They all needed to be in perfect alignment.

"Hut two three four, hut two three four." The drill instructors barked these commands in deep staccato repetition. When we were expected to deviate from our previous movements, they drew out the word before the new command, which sounded almost like a howl, perhaps to get our attention.

"To the rear, march."

"Hut two three four, hut two three four."

"Squadron, halt."

It was hard to imagine Air Force pilots marching to war in a formation, but I guessed that it was part of developing teamwork and discipline. I was always a good follower, so I did okay the first year.

In 1964, anti-Vietnam War demonstrations were heating up at the university. ROTC cadets were prime targets for the wrath of demonstrators. They carried signs:

Out of Vietnam

Infidel

Baby Killer

Murderer

Fascist Pigs

I could never win a verbal confrontation with one of them. It would be impossible to justify my reasons for wearing a military uniform when the military was being accused of killing babies in Vietnam.

The first semester, I was stuck with wearing my Air Force uniform as I walked past demonstrators to both my English and history classes. I could sense that students, and even some professors, were viewing me with an evil eye. I made it through the semester with little direct confrontation, but for the second semester there needed to be a change. I needed to be sure I had an open period before and after each ROTC drill class so I could change into and out of my uniform. With extra time, I could then walk the back streets to the drill class building. Maybe I could avoid their swearing and spitting.

My second semester grades were a little better than the first semester. I was proud of the fact that I had now completed one year of college, and that next year, if I decided to continue, I could be a sophomore. If I had to go back to farming, I would at least have the satisfying feeling that I tried to become a fighter pilot.

LOVE, MARRIAGE,
AND HEARTBREAK

I broke up with my high school sweetheart a couple of years prior to going to college while I was still on the farm. To be perfectly honest, she initiated the breakup with me. I suspected she was influenced by her father, the pastor. I did not pass the smell test as being suitable for his daughter. He evidently wanted his daughter to marry some well-spoken, college educated, culturally correct young man, not some incoherent farm kid who slept during his sermons and smelled like cow manure.

A short time later, I met a farm girl who lived about five miles up the road from my house. I always knew about her, but I did not know her directly because she attended a different high school. A local farmer had built a new barn, and to celebrate its completion, he threw a barn dance party with live music. Of course, there was beer. John, my closest friend, and I could never miss out on a good party. After drinking a few beers, my attention became focused on a beautiful girl standing at the end of the bar. I was somewhat good at carrying on a conversation with girls, so I abandoned John and went over and started talking to her. She also had been drinking a few beers, so John and I drove her home that night. I kissed her forehead and said good night, wondering if she would ever want to see me again. Sandy later said she was attracted to me because of my big blue eyes from my German heritage.

When I was away at college the first year, we communicated with each other via letters. Occasionally, John would bring her to the university and drive us around while we sat in the back seat and chatted. During spring break, I got to spend some time together with her at the home of one of her relatives. We developed a close-knit bond and had the same goals. We could provide moral support to each other to get through college. She would make the perfect wife, so I asked her to marry me. She accepted.

John and I still maintained close contact with each other. We were third cousins, grew up as next-door farm neighbors, and had a lot of the same interests. We enjoyed all types of fast racing—whether it was participating in side-by-side drag racing on the county road with our dad's cars, or watching modified race cars, dragsters, or midgets. He bought a go-cart, souped-up the engine, and modified the chassis. This go-cart was a fast racing type, not like the kind you pay to ride at an amusement park. With its power, the front wheels raised into the air when you floored the gas pedal.

John was kind enough to let me drive his go-cart. Drivers at this paved racetrack were required to wear a shoulder harness and a helmet. I strapped in, put on the helmet, and stomped on the gas pedal. It was exhilarating to feel the initial acceleration, then to go around curves sideways, and to feel the power coming out of curves rocketing me forward up to forty miles per hour on the straight away. I slid around the first few curves okay. But the next curve caused a problem. Instead of sliding around it, the go-cart rear wheel struck a loose chunk of asphalt on the track and flipped. The inverted go-cart pushed me headfirst into some gravel off the side of the track. Somewhat shaken, I got out of the upside-down go-cart, stood up, and unfastened my helmet chinstrap. My friend and several others saw what happened and ran to help me.

"I'm okay," I assured them.

"No, you're not."

I put my hand up to my face and felt a warm gooey liquid; I looked at my hand and it was blood red. I was having a little trouble focusing my left eye.

They helped me into John's truck.

"We are taking you to the hospital."

The hospital was ten miles away and the ride seemed to take an eternity. John handed me a towel so I would not get blood all over his truck. I was starting to get a little anxious because I wanted to know how bad this was. He would not let me look in the rearview mirror. At the hospital, they took me directly into the emergency room where the doctor extracted a three-quarter inch chunk of gravel from my chin and sewed up a one inch long cut just above my left eye. A fraction of an inch lower and I would have lost my eye. There are no one-eyed fighter pilots in the US Air Force.

Sandy knew that I had not yet told my parents about our upcoming marriage. When she first saw my bandaged face without knowing it was a racing accident, she thought the worst had happened, that Dad beat me up because I was getting married. It could not be further from the truth. Dad had never laid a hand on me. In fact, when I told him, he was elated about our upcoming marriage.

The wedding consisted of a church ceremony and a get together at the farm. We planned to keep the party small, so none of the neighbors were invited, or at least that is what I thought. After the church ceremony, our wedding party returned to Ma and Dad's farmhouse for some snacks and beer. We were sitting in the kitchen having a nice peaceful conversation when I was alarmed by loud noises and hollering from outside the farmhouse.

"George, George, we want to party! Beer money, we want beer money. C'mon George, give us some money."

I did not have any money.

"George, George, money, or we take the bride. Hand over money now!"

I poked my head out the door and recognized the noisy people as my neighbors, so I decided to play along for a while. The noise got louder and louder as they rang cowbells, lit fireworks, fired shotguns, beeped horns, hooted, and hollered. They wanted to be part of the party. Dad just happened to be standing beside me with some money for them. I found out later that he knew about this all along. It was planned so the neighbors could be part of our wedding celebration. It was an old tradition called a chivaree. The neighbors bought a keg of beer, I got to keep my bride, and everybody partied together. It made me feel sort of special.

Sandy and I planned a short honeymoon to the northern part of the state. Ma and Dad let us use their car for the long drive to a campground where the fishing was supposed to be good. My roommate friend from the university joined us for one night in the tent. We caught some fish and were getting ready to clean them for supper when he accidently dropped all of them back into the lake, so there went our supper. Since we now had no fish, we had to guess on canned food that had no labels because of a prank by my sisters. It turned out to be beans, not exactly a desirable honeymoon food item.

Sandy and I had a joyous time on our honeymoon. The radio was cranked up to WLS in Chicago as we were driving home on a main highway in Dad's '61 Chevy. We were only twenty miles from home when we were suddenly jolted by a severe impact. Our car was spun around in the road, and the force pushed us into a ditch. Sandy and I were shaken, but otherwise uninjured. The driver of the car that hit us had gone through a stop sign, and he slammed into the driver's side rear quarter panel of our car. I jumped out of our car and ran full speed to try and confront him, but he sped off. I ran back to the driver of another car who had witnessed the accident and asked him if he would follow that guy to get his license plate number. He came back a short time later.

"The car is in the ditch about a mile down the road. The driver is slumped over the steering wheel. When I walked up to see if he was okay, he had a strong smell of alcohol."

A nearby farmer heard the collision and called the police. We directed the officers to the location of the drunk and police records later showed that they arrested him. I never heard about any further consequences, but he was probably released from jail after sobering up and went about his merry ways without any legal ramifications. It once again highlighted the consequences from overindulgence in alcohol. A split-second sooner, and he would have impacted my driver's side door.

I was pleased to be well liked by folks who lived close to Dad's farm. They were cordial relatives, long-time acquaintances of Dad, and classmates from my one-room grade school with whom I had bonded for several years. When I was home for the summer, they asked sincere questions that indicated a true interest in finding out what I was doing.

"George, what courses are you taking at the university? Are you going back next year? What will you do after you graduate?"

My demanding university studies sapped much of my socialization capability. My relationship with other hometown locals became increasingly strained when I could not remember their names. Some were a part of the pee in the bottle stunt, so they avoided me. I hoped that maybe they were feeling some remorse for having belittled me. I patronized the area taverns with my new father-in-law where some patrons pretended to want to talk to me.

"George, what are you doing around here? I thought you were this bigshot academic guy. Are you going to stay home for good now and help your dad?"

"I don't know yet. I am still considering whether or not I'll go back to school next year," I usually told them.

Since I was not an entertaining conversationalist, they either wandered off to a distant seat at the bar, or they turned their attention to my father-in-law to talk about their new tractor, how much milk their cows were producing, the latest pig prices, who quit their job, who died, or who knocked-up some girl in town. They had zero interest in talking about ancient history, Spanish, English, ROTC, or my life at the university. I could not blame them. I avoided any mention of wanting to be a fighter pilot. If I failed, I did not want to be poked fun of for being a failure. My hope was that someday I could make my hometown folks proud of the accomplishments of one of their boys.

After the wedding, Dad seemed to be under the impression that I would settle down and work the farm to support my new wife. Dad and Ma liked Sandy and were pleased that we would initially be living with them in the farmhouse. Maybe now I would get back to the routine of milking cows and doing fieldwork on the farm as he originally planned. Dad had always thought I was destined to keep the farm homestead in the family so that it would someday be a century farm, meaning 100 years in our family. Several relatives lived in the area with my same last name and they all could trace their roots back to that farm. Dad soon had to face a heartbreaking moment: I was not coming back to the farm.

Dad was getting up in years and without an heir to take over the farm, he had to downsize his operation and load his beloved cows onto a semi-truck destined for market. He sold all the pigs and chickens to a slaughterhouse. The land was rented to a neighbor while he and Ma resided in the farmhouse and made plans to sell the farm and move to town. I was not part of their decision-making process. I cared about the farm but had to focus on my mission to become a fighter pilot and I needed every bit of my mental stamina to achieve that goal.

If I was going to continue my studies at the university, I needed money, so I took a summer job at the local canning factory. My job was to make brine, a steaming saltwater that was injected into each can of peas just before the can was sealed. I had to fill large vats with water, dump fifty-pound bags of salt into the vats, and then start the steamer. The rest of the time I either sat around doing nothing, or I went downstairs to visit with the old ladies who were working on the pea belt line. They removed vines, stems, and worms from the peas as they rolled along on a slow-moving canvas belt. They got excited when they found a worm because they got a reward for it. I had a good relationship with them, and I knew many of them from my time growing up near the town. They seemed to respect me for what I was doing—going to college, that is, not making brine.

ANXIETY AND DEPRESSION

Sandy also wanted to get a college degree and that was a big factor in my reason for returning to college. We needed to find a place to live in the university town, but we also needed food, a car, and money. Ma, Dad, and Sandy's parents helped us with an occasional offering of meat, eggs, milk, vegetables, and some other staples, but the university was an hour drive from the farm so it was not feasible to go back and forth to stock up on supplies. It was also prohibitive to spend time away from our studies. We bought a used Volkswagen car. It raised eyebrows when we drove it back home because foreign cars were laughed at by the locals. Admittedly, the car was a piece of crap. Several times during the cold winter months when we had to get to class, it would not start. I never wanted to miss classes because I might fail to get some critical lecture information that was needed for taking a test. I sometimes had to take the bus or pay lots of money for a cab. With a shortage of money, the cab was a last resort because it meant cutting back on some necessities like laundry, soap, deodorant, or food. Getting through college was the priority.

Even though we had little money, I could not justify working more than part-time as a gas station attendant and, during the summer, as a lumber yard worker. We learned that we were eligible for grants and loans for living expenses and found a subsidized low-income apartment in a seedy part of town. New neighbors came and went, sometimes making it a better place to live, other times not. And police visits to the area were a common occurrence. We qualified for this place because of our income. It was almost zero.

Nights and weekends were devoted to studying. Since I did not have good study habits, I needed to study, study, study. My attention span was short. I could read twenty pages of *War and Peace*, and then suddenly realize that my mind was wandering, and I was not comprehending anything I was reading. I did a lot of highlighting and note-taking. Writing notes seemed to help my unfocused brain absorb information. Sometimes it seemed like I was rewriting just about everything I was reading.

There was always a possibility I could flunk out of college because there were still challenging courses to be completed. I now had some choice of courses that were not as boring as Spanish and English grammar. I enrolled in geology because the professor was supposedly entertaining, but he was known to be a hard grader. One of his lectures was devoted to the origins of neolithic and paleolithic man. He not only talked about them; he walked across the stage and acted out their posture by bending over and hunching his back with his arms dangling, sort of like Quasimodo in the *Hunchback of Notre Dame.* He interjected occasional grunting sounds that imitated a monkey and the class roared with laughter. It was probably my only class at the university that had any joviality. I got an A in geology. Mathematics was one of my strengths and I even took calculus. Climatology and meteorology were interesting courses because they had practical applications.

The time was nearing for that dreaded speech to the ROTC class. I chose the subject for my presentation to be UFO's (Unidentified Flying Objects). The instructor, a captain, told me that if I could convince him that aliens existed, he would give me an A. I spent a lot of time at the library researching Project Blue Book which was a UFO investigative agency within the Air Force. Most UFOs were explainable as natural phenomena such as swamp gasses, reflecting lights, hallucinations, or people trying to get attention with some man-made object. One unexplainable UFO crashed in Roswell, New Mexico in 1947. I focused on that incident to develop my argument that aliens did visit the earth.

I had built up a lot of anxiety over the speech and it was now time to do it. I tried to look confident while making my way to the front of the class. My knees were a little shaky, but I could stand behind a lectern, so maybe nobody would notice. Thank goodness I was permitted to use three by five-inch note cards, so I did not have to memorize the presentation. I started to speak. Words came out of my mouth. My opening line was humorous, although I had not planned it that way. The instructor smiled, and some students even laughed. My comfort level increased, and I enjoyed seeing the focused look on faces in the audience. The presentation flowed incredibly well, and when it was over, I not only felt relief, but great satisfaction for doing it without any screw-ups. The captain commented that he was not convinced about the existence of aliens, but my speech was worthy of an A.

Good news about the speech was followed by bad news about the AFOQT. I passed the basic test but failed the aviation part. I would be given one chance to retake it after 150 days. I found out from some other cadets who passed the test that there was a study guide from which I could learn about potential aviation questions on the test. Had I known about it before taking the test the first time, I may have passed it.

My ROTC instructor was a disgruntled Air Force captain who had washed out of pilot training and was stuck in his position until he completed his service commitment. He liked many of the ROTC students, especially those he found entertaining, but there were some he did not like, and I fell within that group. Having to deal with me seemed to be a waste of his time. To be accepted into the advanced ROTC program as a junior, I had to go through an interview with a panel of officers that included this captain, plus two majors and a colonel. During this interview, I had to convince them about why I should be an Air Force officer and a fighter pilot.

The interview was both disheartening and motivating for me. The captain tried to discourage me from pursuing any ambitions in the US Air Force. He was blunt. I did not fit the mold of a good Air Force officer. Since I could not pass the aviation part of the AFOQT, I would never make it through pilot training, much less be a fighter pilot.

The demeaning comments, test failures, difficulties with studies, and my recognition that I lacked social skills were starting to get me depressed.

What did I do wrong in life that requires me to endure these difficulties? Why can't I be intelligent, like that super smart fellow who doesn't believe in God? Why can't I be charismatic like many of the other cadets so people will like me? Why can't I be authoritative, so my instructor respects me?

My daydreaming mind wandered into alternative options to the Air Force. Maybe the Navy's standards were less stringent. Then again, the Navy was water oriented, so they probably required their recruits to know how to swim. I did not know how to swim, so the Navy was ruled out. The Army would take just about anybody and you did not need a commission to be a pilot. However, they did not fly fighter jets. Flying low and slow in propeller driven airplanes or helicopters did not seem attractive to me. If all else failed, the Army could be a last resort where I could at least fly airplanes. When I was further down in the dumps, there was the thought about just giving up on everything and going back to Dad's farm.

This captain evidently did not understand (or maybe he did) that there was power in negative motivation. Like a switch that flipped in my mind, I became mentally combative and decided that nothing could stop me from pursuing my goals in the Air Force. I wanted to prove this captain wrong; and I cherished the thought of returning to that ROTC office someday after becoming a fighter pilot, confronting him about his horrible prediction, and somehow, shoving it up his butt.

Classes in college were getting easier because I could now select more elective courses. I focused on courses that were the most interesting and easiest for me. I had to declare a major and since I had the most credits in geography courses, it became my major. For the Air Force it did not matter what I chose for a major.

DREADED PHYSICAL

I received good news in the summer between my sophomore and junior year. I passed the AFOQT aviation test and was selected for upper classman status in the ROTC program. To be considered for pilot training, I had to undergo an extensive flight physical by the Air Force medical clinic. It included an eye exam, EKG, hearing test, a physical, and dental exam. Pilot candidates needed to be in nearly perfect health with 20/20 eyesight, normal hearing, no physical abnormalities, and no history of major problems in the family. Any episodes of unexplainable unconsciousness, major injuries, seizures, psychological disorders, or other significant ailments would be grounds for elimination. I worried a little about passing the exam with my neck whiplash, farm injuries, and history of leg pains, but otherwise felt confident about my physical condition. After all, I was a farm kid.

First stop at the clinic was the blood draw. I hated needles from my numerous visits to Dr. Sharp when I was a kid. He always seemed to have a shot for anything that ailed me. The needle insertion went okay. Then I looked down at that long needle sticking in my arm with a seemingly humongous vial attached to the end of it. That was a mistake. My red blood was slowly oozing into that vial. When one was full, there was another one. I started to feel lightheaded.

"How many more of those before you are done?" I asked the nurse.

When the blood draw was finally complete, I immediately went into a stall in the bathroom, closed the door, puked, sat on the toilet lid, and passed out. My subconscious mind told me not to fall off the toilet seat or it would bring unwanted attention to myself. I never told anybody about this.

Numerous fillings in my teeth were concerning to the Air Force dentist. When I was a kid, Ma forced me to go to Dr. Moen every six months, and he always found ten or more cavities. The cavities were thought to be the result of soft teeth and water from the farm well which did not contain cavity preventing fluoride. I had vivid memories of visits to Dr Moen. I loved to exaggerate my dental visits because it helped to retain my sanity. Right after I was seated in his plastic covered chair, he shoved a tray in front of me to show off his torture tools. There were picks, drill bits, a little round mirror, clamps, air hose nozzle, spittoon, an incredibly long-needled syringe, and lots of cotton swabs to soak up all the expected blood. I think I may have even seen a hammer and chisel. For the cavities in my front teeth, he grabbed his syringe, squirted a little juice up in the air in front of me so I could see what he was about to do, stabbed the needle into my gum, shoved it up into the roof of my mouth and then wiggled it around. It felt like he was pushing it into the upper chambers of my nostril. Perhaps he was trying to numb my brain as well as my teeth. After he determined that my upper lip was numb by stabbing his metal pick into it to see if I would jump, he then started his detestable drilling. He always hit nerves that he obviously missed with his numbing stuff. Every time he hit a live nerve, I twitched, and groaned. After several visits to this guy, I thought I could outsmart him by groaning, twitching, and jerking before he hit a nerve in order to get him to load me up with more of the numbing stuff. It only worked a couple of times before he figured out my antics.

For my back teeth, there was no numbing; he just grabbed his slow noisy drill.

As the drill screeched, an awful smell of something burning permeated the air, and particles of tooth-dust flew into my eyes. When he finally put his drill down, he grabbed his metal pick to chip away at the hole he had just created. He was still not done. He went for his powered auger again, but this time he replaced the head on it with a bullet shaped grinding wheel.

When he finally let me spit, I stuck my tongue into the humongous hole he had just created in my tooth. I tried to anticipate when the end was near, but he always seemed to find one more tooth on which to do his dastardly deed.

When he stood in front of me with his legs spread apart, bad thoughts crossed my mind about how I could get him to stop. He finally stopped when he was evidently satisfied that he had inflicted enough pain. He showed little mercy for the squirming kid in his chair. I started breathing normally when he finally told his assistant to mix up the cement to fill the holes. Those hours of pain I endured in Dr Moen's chair were now worth it when the Air Force dentist determined that my teeth met the minimum standards.

One evening, while studying in our apartment, I started feeling some minor discomfort in my lower abdomen. It progressed from minor to severe to brutal to unbearable. There was no body position that would help to ease the pain. It was so bad that I ended up on the floor in the fetal position crying, moaning, and puking. After a few hours, the pain started to subside, and I went into the bathroom to urinate. My urine was blood red. Something was drastically wrong. I could not hide nor ignore this problem; I had to go to a doctor to find out what was wrong.

The university offered free medical care to students. I was first examined by a medical student who had no clue about what caused my pain. A real doctor then examined me and ordered some tests. Doctors always needed to do tests before they could offer a diagnosis, so I provided him his required urine sample. The urine test result came back with evidence of blood so at least the doctor was convinced that I was telling the truth. He sent me to radiology for some x-rays of the lower abdomen. After several hours of waiting for the results, I was informed that the tests did not reveal any problems. He sent me home with some pain pills and scheduled me for another test two days later. The IVP (intravenous pyelogram) test would do nothing to solve my problem, but it would help this doctor satisfy his paperwork requirements. It probably did not matter to him that I had a fear of needles and he was making me undergo an intravenous injection of sickening iodine contrast dye, which made me puke. Dad's treatment of farm animals was better than this.

I continued to pass more red urine and there was another episode of the terrible pain in the lower left area of my abdomen. The IVP revealed the definitive cause for the pain as a kidney stone. There was nothing the doctor could do for me except prescribe pain medication. The stone had to travel its natural course out of my kidney, through my ureter, bladder, and urethra. I was advised to drink lots of liquids. The thought that this stone was going to exit through my penis hurt almost as bad as the actual pain.

The doctor wanted to determine the composition of the stone, so I had to pee into a strainer to catch it when it passed. There was a burning sensation and then a feeling of some sharp lump passing through my penis. After the stone passed, my entire body seemed to go into a relaxed state of relief. I tried to make light of the situation by telling Sandy that it was a humongous rock. She stared at me and I could tell what she was thinking.

Just another one of his sick jokes.

Air Force pilots had to undergo a flight physical annually. I now had to worry about another thing. First, I had the unconsciousness from the blood draw, and now this kidney stone condition. How would this episode affect my chances of becoming a fighter pilot?

SUMMER CAMP

In the summer between my junior and senior year, I had to attend a month-long ROTC camp at an active duty Air Force base. The Air Force issued summer uniforms plus all the gear and supplies. I was looking forward to wearing that uniform because it presented me as a member of the United States Air Force.

My friend from high school accompanied me on the twenty-nine-hour drive to the base. The first mistake I made when I got there was when I stepped out of his car.

"Cadet Kohn, get off the grass. You do not ever walk on the commander's grass. Now get your gear, and get your ass to your room, pronto."

Oh boy, this is going to be interesting.

I could not even say thanks or goodbye to my friend.

Mornings at the camp began with a wake-up call to the sounds of a screechy bugle playing reveille, followed by booming commands from the instructors.

"Cadets, get out of bed now. Let's get going. Move it, move it, move it. We don't have all day. Assemble outside at oh five fifteen. Cadet Kohn, you better get your ass in gear."

Maybe Ma had unknowingly prepared me for this rude awakening when she tried to get me out of bed in the morning on the farm. Ma never raised her voice in anger. She only did it for emphasis. Dad's words of scolding when I showed up in a sleepy daze in the barn were not harsh,

74

just emphatic. Even if Ma and Dad had a disagreement, it never resulted in hollering or exchanges of mean words. This now was my indoctrination into angry-sounding military discipline.

Cadets were randomly selected to lead the group in calisthenics. One cadet was chosen as group commander and other cadets were chosen to lead each of the ten squadrons. The leaders were given artificial military rank of cadet colonel for group commander; and either cadet major or cadet captain for squadron leaders; all others were cadet lieutenants. The positions rotated on a weekly basis so that each cadet was given a chance to occupy a command position to demonstrate leadership capability.

Everything we did at that camp needed to be done in accordance with strict standards. Clothes had to be hung in the closet with one inch spacing between hangars.

"Cadet Kohn, the space between your hangars is one and one-fourth inches. Here is a ruler. Now see if you can get it right."

The instructor probably could not tell the difference between one inch and one and one-fourth inches on the hangars, but he needed to harass me. Beds needed to be made with the green army blanket covers tucked in on the corners at an exact forty-five-degree angle. The instructor acted like he was measuring it with a protractor.

"Cadet Kohn, this bed corner is not even close to a forty-five-degree angle. Now do it over and I will be back to check it."

Bed covers needed to be so tight that when the instructor dropped a coin on the bed, the coin would bounce in the air.

"Cadet Kohn, can't you do anything right?"

I found it nearly impossible to get a bed cover that tight, but I did it over anyway.

Much of the time at camp was spent in classes learning military protocol, and in touring the base. Everywhere we went, we marched in formation.

"Group," the cadet group commander hollered.

"Squadron," the cadet squadron commanders echoed.

"A-ten-shun!"

Cadets popped to attention.

"Forward . . ." The commander would draw out the sound for a few seconds before asserting the order: "March."

Everyone proceeded in step to the cadence.

"Hut, two, three, four."

"Hut, two, three, four."

Cadets were encouraged to get creative with the cadence.

"Birdie, birdie in the sky,

Dropped some whitewash in my eye.

I don't complain and I don't cry,

I'm just glad that cows can't fly.

Left, left, left, your right, your left."

Those big silver airplanes parked on the tarmac with *AIR FORCE* on the side were a beautiful sight that got me excited. I wanted to get into the cockpit and go fly right then and there. I was confident I could learn how to do it. After all, I learned how to drive a tractor and operate big machinery on the farm. The adrenalin was pumping, and I could not wait to get started on my next steps toward becoming a fighter pilot.

After a month of summer camp harassment, I was back home at the university when the ROTC instructor tasked me to lead a day-long formation training exercise for about fifty underclassmen. I recognized that it was a test to determine if I had the leadership qualities to be an Air Force officer. I worried that the captain instructor was setting me up to fail by overloading me with a nearly impossible task. I decided to prove to him that I could do it. There was plenty of time to prepare and mentally rehearse my training scenarios. First, I had all the underclassmen cadets assemble in the bleachers while I stood out front verbalizing and demonstrating the first of several formation marching procedures. Then, I commanded the cadets to expeditiously move out of the bleachers, fall into formation, and stand at attention. They needed to keep their chin up, chest out, shoulders back, stomach in, and heels together. Their eyes better be fixated straight ahead. It was fun to test a few by standing off to the side while talking to them to see if their eyes followed me. I inspected their haircuts, uniforms, and shoeshines, then had them practice basic formation movements, such as marching forward and halting, as well as executing more specific commands, like *column left, column right, to the rear*, and *about face*. I had enough maneuvers planned to take up the entire day. I felt comfortable doing this, and even a little cocky bellowing out commands and strutting among the cadets to correct any missteps. My thorough preparation resulted in the exercises flowing seamlessly from one event to the next. Throughout the entire ordeal, I had two goals in mind: to teach these underclassmen the basics of military formations, and, more importantly, to earn respect from the instructors. Hopefully, the captain, two majors and a colonel, who were standing by to take over in case I failed, saw that many cadets came up to shake my hand when it was over.

Senior cadets in the ROTC program who were designated to enter pilot training after graduation were enrolled in an introductory aviation training course. One of the ROTC instructors was an Air Force pilot who taught a ground school course that ended with the Federal Aviation Administration (FAA) written test. I liked this instructor and thought maybe he liked me too because I had mentored his wife who was in a college course that we were both enrolled in at the university.

Flight training consisted of thirty hours in a Cessna 172 high wing, single-engine, propeller-type aircraft at a local Fixed Base Operation (FBO). One trainee on a solo mission completed all his exterior preflight checks, got into the airplane, started it up, and remembered that he forgot something. He left the aircraft engine running while he ran inside the FBO to get whatever he forgot. His civilian instructor saw this and reported him to our ROTC instructor. It was determined that he had demonstrated poor judgement. He was busted out of the Cessna 172 training, and disenrolled from the pathway to Air Force pilot training. I could easily have done the same thing and was thankful it was not me.

Forty hours of flight instruction was required to qualify for an FAA private pilot's license. I decided to pay for an additional ten hours. I had to take a checkride with an FAA designated check airman. He was a grumpy old curmudgeon who seemed to relish the fact that he was in command over a critical aspect of someone's life. I had to ignore his surly mannerisms and focus on flying the airplane. I passed the checkride and was awarded a private pilot's license.

I told the Air Force that I would graduate from college in June, and then realized that I was six credits short of the number needed to graduate. The Air Force had an age cutoff of twenty-seven for entering pilot training so I could not dilly-dally around. Age was a factor because I had spent two years after high school working on the farm before starting college. I enrolled in two easy summer school courses and revised my graduation date to August. Getting that Bachelor of Science degree from the university was a huge relief knowing that I had completed the first big step toward becoming a fighter pilot.

I was required to attend a commissioning ceremony in Class A uniform at which time I would be awarded a commission as a second lieutenant in the United States Air Force. I was filled with excitement. Sandy, Ma, and Dad were there. The colonel commander of the ROTC unit made a few opening remarks at the start of the ceremony, and then asked an unexpected question.

"Have any of you had a change in your medical condition since your last physical?"

My mind was racing.

Oh shit. Make up your mind fast, George. Should I, or shouldn't I raise my hand?

I knew that the Air Force had permission to dig into any aspect of my history, so they could certainly check my university medical records and find out that I had a kidney stone. Integrity was a key character trait for Air Force officers. If I were caught not revealing information, it would result in getting kicked out. I reluctantly raised my hand. The colonel responded disgustedly as if he did not want to hear from me.

"Yes, Cadet Kohn."

"Sir, I had a kidney stone."

The colonel laughed disparagingly.

"Cadet Kohn. I do not think that is a problem," he smirked.

This colonel obviously knew nothing about the effects of kidney stones on a pilot's career. He made me feel foolish for truthfully answering his question. He made it obvious that he was not going to recognize me as a fellow officer who deserved to be treated with dignity and respect. Why did he need to be so cruel as to belittle me in front of my proud family members? I struggled to maintain my smile, but the hurt penetrated deep inside. It was not how I wanted to start my career in the Air Force.

"Cadets, raise your right hand and repeat after me:"

"I, George William Kohn, having been appointed a second lieutenant, United States Air Force, do solemnly swear that I will support and defend the constitution of the United States against all enemies, foreign and domestic; that I will bear true faith and allegiance to the same; that I take this obligation freely, without any mental reservation or purpose of evasion; and that I will well and faithfully discharge the duties of the office upon which I am about to enter, *so help me God.*"

The ROTC captain, who was previously my antagonist, pinned a gold bar onto the left shoulder of my new class A blue Air Force uniform. Sandy pinned the gold bar on my right shoulder, and I was now an officer in the United States Air Force.

Military tradition was that a new officer was encouraged to give a two-dollar bill to the first person who saluted him. The military salute is a greeting from one military person to another; plus, it is also a sign of respect for the position. Historians believe the salute originated in Roman times when assassinations were common. If a Roman citizen wanted to see a public official, he had to approach with his right hand raised to show that he was not holding a weapon.

A master sergeant from the ROTC office staff knew the tradition and was ready and waiting. He popped a smart salute. I responded back with an equally smart salute, reached into my pocket, and presented him with a two-dollar bill. The tradition was supposed to symbolize good luck for my Air Force career.

PART THREE

LOFTY GOAL

I was off to a Texas base for Air Force pilot training. Sandy and our young son, Paul, would be joining me later as she was finishing her studies at the university. The Air Force had family housing available for us in a two-bedroom unfurnished duplex on base. I loved living on base where I could hear the roar of those powerful jet engines and watch the sleek silver and white jets taking off and landing throughout the day. Formations of airplanes flew overhead. Each aircraft peeled out of formation at precise intervals by flicking their wings nearly vertical into a steep banked turn to circle back for landing. Their precision was as impressive as any synchronized Olympic event. I felt a tickle of excitement in my heart.

I could be doing that someday.

The first few days of class consisted of listening to briefings and completing paperwork. Every document needed to be completed in a precise manner: sign only in black ink; the date is always written as day, month, and then year, with no abbreviations; and time is always expressed by the twenty-four-hour clock because there is no *a.m.* or *p.m.* in the military. Emphasis was on the military way of doing things with no deviation from standard procedures. There were briefings by finance for pay and allowances, CBPO (Central Base Personnel Office) for life insurance beneficiaries and personal records, base billeting for housing arrangements, medical for hospital benefits, the chaplain for religious affiliations, and whoever else wanted to talk. They provided necessary information, but I was anxious to get going with flying airplanes.

The Air Force issued each of us three flight suits. They resembled coveralls with a top zipper that closed at the front and a bottom zipper that opened the lower part of the flight suit so guys could take a leak. There were no women in Air Force pilot training, not that it would have made any difference in the uniform. The flight suit had pockets on the arms, chest, thighs, and legs. The arm pockets were often used for storing a pack of cigarettes, plus there were slots for pens and pencils. The chest pockets were for wallets and other personal items, and the leg pockets were stuffed with checklists and flight briefing cards. I felt a lot of pride every time I stepped into that flight suit.

My pilot training class started with one-hundred students. It was made known early on that the *wash out* rate from pilot training was high.

"Look to your left. Now look to your right. One of those two will not be here at graduation."

Relationships initially were distant because a friend today may be a goner tomorrow. The class was divided in half with an *A* flight scheduled for morning ground school and afternoon flight training and vice versa for a *B* flight. The schedules flipped every week.

The class had a mix of personalities from various localities throughout the United States. One fellow was from Mississippi, and he was interesting because he spoke with a heavy southern drawl. A few had fathers in the Air Force, so they already knew the military routine. Many guys were good conversationalists, so they started to bond early on. I belonged to the category of the quiet and humorless ones. I occasionally made feeble attempts at socializing, but as I hadn't done much of that during my upbringing on the farm, I usually failed miserably. Fortunately for me, personality was not a factor in success or failure in pilot training. In or out was based solely on whether you could fly airplanes in accordance with Air Force standards.

Ground school initially consisted of T-41 aircraft systems, limitations, and procedures. The T-41 was the military designation for the civilian Cessna 172, the same type of aircraft that I had flown to get my private pilot's license. Engine, fuel, avionics, and electrical were all taught in one week and the student was required to know every intricate detail of the airplane. Bold-faced emergency procedures were memory items that we were expected to recite verbatim when the time came. It was an intense learning process.

T-41 flight training was conducted by civilian flight instructors at an FBO (fixed base operation) at the local civilian airport. In the flight training room, students were seated around old wooden tables. A daily routine was for an instructor to stand in front of the class, ask a question about the airplane, and then point to a trainee for an answer. There were always questions that could stump somebody.

I liked these question and answer sessions because it provided me with an outlet for demonstrating my knowledge. I always knew the answer to a question when the instructor called on me. When a classmate could not answer a question, I often raised my hand.

"Does anyone know all the documents that must be on board the aircraft prior to flight?" the instructor might ask.

I had memorized the list. My hand would shoot up.

"Yes, Lt. Kohn."

"Sir, weight and balance, airworthiness certificate, aircraft registration, flight crew checklist, pilot aid, and applicable airport information."

"Very good, Lt. Kohn."

My struggles through the early years of college were not because of a deficiency in intelligence, they were due to a lack of good study habits. I overcame that, and I became good at memorizing long lists of items and retaining subject matter. I earned respect from my classmates, but I feared that it was an envious type of respect. We all knew that it was important to not only graduate from pilot training, but to graduate at the top of the class. It was hard not to feel a slight tinge of joy whenever a classmate screwed up. We were competing against each other. Only the top students got assignments to fly fighter jets.

For the flight training, students were expected to fly a precise flight path paralleling a four-lane highway to a training area. There were lots of airplanes heading to and from the training area. Various maneuvers were practiced. On return to the airport, students needed to check in with tower controllers over a designated checkpoint for permission to land. Instructors were not there to hold your hand or babysit you, either you put out the effort to learn the information and do it correctly, or you were out. There were checkrides to evaluate your knowledge and ability.

My previous training and experience in the Cessna 172 gave me a slight advantage. Some students had never flown an airplane. The strict requirement to adhere to procedures, and the required hand-eye coordination necessary to fly an airplane under a fast-paced learning regimen caused some to quit. Quitting was called SIE (self-imposed elimination) and the Air Force did not look kindly on quitters. They assigned them to a mediocre desk job so that they could fulfill their four-year commitment.

Some washouts had a strong desire to fly, but they were pukers. Puking on one flight was expected, but not puking on every flight. If they were puking, they could not fly the airplane, so they lost valuable hands-on flying time. They were advised to find another vocation in the Air Force. About 20 percent of the class washed out of the T-41 phase. I passed the final T-41 checkride, so it was on to the next phase of pilot training.

The T-37 was a twin-engine jet trainer. A combat version of the T-37 was the A-37. The *T* meant it was a trainer; the *A* meant it was an attack aircraft. It was frequently employed by foreign countries. The South Vietnamese Air Force utilized A-37s as their primary combat aircraft.

The T-37 had a bulbous nose to make room for side by side pilot seating. The fuselage tapered to the rear sort of like a dragonfly. Its turbojet engines had a loud, high-pitched whine, so it was affectionately known as the *tweet*. Sometimes it was jokingly referred to as a 6,000-pound dog whistle, or as a *converter* because it converted air and fuel into noise and smoke.

The flight manual for the T-37 was the *dash one*; every aircraft in the Air Force had a dash one. It contained comprehensive descriptions of the aircraft components, checklists for normal and emergency procedures, limitations, cautions, warnings, and performance charts. Each student was issued the one-inch thick T-37-1 to study, and they were expected to know everything in it.

Students all had to get a flight physical. I worried about the blood draw, but it turned out to be uneventful. Medical personnel asked a lot of questions.

"Ever felt light-headed or dizzy?"

I fibbed. "No."

"Ever had any kidney problems?"

I answered this question honestly; there was no other choice. The university hospital had documented my history of a kidney stone and the Air Force could access those records. I emphasized that it was a singular stone that passed without complication. It was never good to overemphasize any medical condition to a flight surgeon. I did not think that the kidney stone occurrence would be a problem because the ROTC colonel made fun of me when I mentioned it during the commissioning ceremony.

A few days passed and then my instructor told me to report to the squadron commander's office. He was a major in command of the flight instructors and students in my class. It sounded like something serious.

"Lt. Kohn, you are grounded from any further flight training. You need to immediately schedule an appointment to see the flight surgeon," he told me.

All the enthusiasm to become a fighter pilot suddenly drained from my body. I had given up on the farm and worked my butt off to get through college and now this. I suspected what it was about but had to ask anyway.

"Sir, is it the kidney stone?"

"I cannot answer that. Please, just do what I tell you."

There were specific Air Force guidelines for flight surgeons when evaluating various ailments. When I stated that I previously had a kidney stone, the flight surgeon evidently made note of it and did some research. It was not permissible to fly with a kidney stone. Even though I told him that it had passed, that was not good enough. He needed proof that I did not have any more kidney stones in my system.

A kidney stone has sharp protrusions that cut flesh when it moves out of the kidney. If the stone stops moving and blocks the urinary passageway from discharging fluids, the kidney swells and that is what causes tremendous pain. For obvious safety reasons, the Air Force does not want anyone flying an airplane who is experiencing unbearable pain. Even though I had no recurrence of the severe pain that I had in college, this flight surgeon required me to undergo another dreaded IVP. Thankfully, it revealed no kidney stones and I was cleared to resume flight training.

The instructor sat in the right seat and the student in the left seat of the T-37. We wore helmets with oxygen masks. A microphone was incorporated into the oxygen mask so that we could talk between us via an interphone system. The side-by-side seating made it easy for some instructors to physically intimidate a student. They would slap the student aside the helmet, yank on their oxygen mask, or use a stick to rap their knuckles when they made an errant move toward a switch in the cockpit. My instructor was a cordial, mild-mannered fellow who was devoted to teaching. Lt. Bill Tracy was exactly the type of instructor I needed.

Washout rate in the T-37 was higher than in the T-41 because flying a jet airplane was more difficult. The first training flights consisted of learning basic flying skills in a jet trainer. Instructors demonstrated how to fly each maneuver and then the students were expected to do it. Of course, there was an Air Force manual that explained in detail how to perform each training maneuver. It was referred to as a *bible*. Students needed to learn the manual and be proficient in takeoffs and landings, barrel rolls, loops, Immelmanns, lazy eights, chandelles, clover leafs, cuban eights, aileron rolls, single engine approaches to landing, stalls, spins, plus whatever else was in the bible. We would be tested on each of these maneuvers on a checkride.

THE BIG BUST

The offices of check airmen who administered checkrides to students were in a separate building on base. Check airmen held the fate of trainees in their hands. I suspected they segregated this dreaded building from our squadron operations so that the walk to it added to the aura of intimidation. I had to report for my first checkride after seventeen training flights in the T-37. I would be expected to take off and land this complex, high-speed jet airplane, and to be proficient in performing all those aerobatic maneuvers to the satisfaction of a guy who was just sitting there and staring at my every move.

"Sir, Lt. Kohn reporting for a checkride."

"Sit down."

The evaluator was stern looking and direct, creating a tense environment.

"First the oral exam. We will start with *bold face* emergency procedures. I expect you to know them verbatim. Any mistakes and the checkride will be over. Do you understand?"

"Yes, sir."

I had memorized these procedures ad nauseum, but there was no guarantee that I would not get a brain fart and mess up.

"What is the procedure for one engine failure, fire, or overheat during takeoff (after airborne)?"

"Flaps–50 percent; gear–up; flaps–up (one hundred knots indicated airspeed minimum)."

"Tell me the procedure for ejection?"

"Handgrips–raise; triggers–squeeze."

"Give me the procedure for single engine go around."

"Throttle–military; speed brake–in; flaps–50 percent; gear–up; flaps–up (one hundred knots indicated airspeed minimum)."

I got all eight of the bold face procedures right, so it was on to the limitations.

"What is the normal hydraulic pressure range?"

"Twelve fifty to fifteen fifty psi."

"What is the maximum airspeed with the landing lights down?"

"One hundred thirty-five knots indicated airspeed."

"What is the minimum oil pressure at idle?"

"Three psi."

No misses were allowed on limitations questions either. After all, how could a student safely operate an aircraft if they did not know the maximum airspeed, or maximum EGT (exhaust gas temperature) for starting or acceleration?

Then it was on to general aircraft questions. A few misses were permissible, but if there more than a few, the check airman would dig deeper and deeper to determine if you knew the airplane systems. Too many misses could result in a bust.

"Which equipment uses only AC electrical power?"

"Attitude indicator, primary flight instrument lights, hydraulic pressure indicator, fuel flow indicators, oil pressure indicators, and fuel quantity indicator."

"You said attitude indicator. Which one uses only AC?"

He was trying to trick me into making up a wrong answer. I should have said indicators as a plural since they both used AC.

"How are the outboard main gear doors actuated?"

"Hydraulically."

"That is not correct."

Only the inboard gear doors were actuated hydraulically. The outboard gear doors were fastened to the main gear strut and closed when the gear was retracted. It was sort of a trick question since technically the main gear was actuated hydraulically and the gear door attached to it was therefore also hydraulically actuated. I knew this and should have explained it, so it evidently raised some question in the examiner's mind about my knowledge of the systems. He dug deeper and deeper, and this questioning seemed to go on forever. My instructor had previously briefed me to not try and bullshit the evaluator because he knew the aircraft backward and forward. At this point in training, we had only been studying the T-37 for a few weeks but were expected to know all these details. The questioning was intense and stressful, but I passed.

After the oral exam, we walked to our airplane. I made sure to walk on his left side since he was the senior ranking officer. He was stone silent, even though he did not have to be. The thought crossed my mind that he was unhappy with his job, or maybe he was a prick and was just trying to over-exaggerate his status as an evaluator.

I accomplished the walk-around inspection of the exterior of the aircraft with him following close behind to ensure that I did not miss anything. We strapped into the aircraft. I completed the preflight checks of switches, oxygen system, and instruments, then started the two jet engines, taxied, and took off to head for the training area. I could see that he was writing a lot of notes on his knee pad, and it made me worry that he was writing about my screw-ups.

"I want to see a barrel roll."

According to the Air Force Manual 11-249, "a barrel roll is a coordinated roll in which the nose of the aircraft describes a circle around a point on the horizon.

> Step 1: Dive with nose below the reference point.
> Step 2: Wings are level just as the aircraft passes level-flight attitude to the side of the reference point.
> Step 3: Pull and roll until directly above the point.
> Step 4: Continue roll along circular path until inverted level-flight attitude.

Step 5: Be the same distance below the point as you were to the
        side of it."
Step 6: Finish the roll at the same position as in Step 2."

I did the barrel roll somewhat satisfactorily.

"I want to see the stall series."

Stalls consisted of power on, power off, and turning stalls so I had to do all three. A stall occurs when there is separation of airflow over the wing of the aircraft. It was easy to get the plane into a stall. To recover, I just had to unload the aircraft by pushing the stick forward and then applying full power.

"Show me a spin. I will tell you when to recover."

A spin is a violent aircraft maneuver. Pilot's heads are flung back and forth, lateral G forces are straining the body, and loose objects are flying around in the cockpit. The airplane is no longer flying normally; it is spinning like a top around an imaginary vertical axis while plunging toward the ground. In normal flying, aircraft rarely get into a spin, but the Air Force required spin training to learn the proper recovery techniques.

I pulled the throttles to idle and sucked the stick back to my gut as the airspeed bled off. At the first sign of a stall, I jammed down one of the rudders. The nose of the aircraft went down, came back up again and the aircraft started to rotate horizontally about an imaginary axis.

"Recover."

AFM (Air Force Manual) 11-249 recovery procedure is to:

1. "Abruptly apply full rudder opposite the direction of the spin.
2. One turn after applying recovery rudder, abruptly move the stick full forward.
3. As the nose pitches down near the vertical, neutralize the elevator while continuing to hold the rudder until spinning has stopped.
4. After the rotation is definitely stopped, neutralize the rudder and recover from the ensuing dive."

I accomplished these steps in the exact order, or so I thought. The aircraft kept spinning and plunging toward the ground. We were fast descending to the minimum recovery altitude of 10,000 feet where the aircraft had to be recovered from the spin, or the pilots were required to eject.

"I have the aircraft."

It was never a good sign when an evaluator had to take command of the aircraft. I felt a big lump in my throat. I had obviously screwed up. At that point in a checkride, the evaluator usually flew the aircraft back to the base, signaling that the checkride was over. I felt a slim ray of hope when he returned control of the aircraft to me for the next maneuver, which was engine out approach and landing. By now, I was a mental mess, so that maneuver was far from satisfactory.

It seemed to take an eternity to get back to the base.

"Not much to debrief, Lieutenant. The checkride is a bust."

I was given a pink slip to take back to my instructor. This was likely going to be the end of the road for my dream of ever becoming a fighter pilot.

"I busted the checkride. I could not get the airplane out of a spin. I am sure that I did what I was supposed to do. It just would not come out of the spin," I told the instructor.

It was the end of the day and thankfully most of the other students had already left, so the only people in the room were my instructor and myself. I then went into this sob story.

"Dad raised me to be a farmer. Ma did not want me to do this military thing. I was supposed to take over the family farm, but I had this dream of becoming an Air Force fighter pilot. I had to struggle to get through college."

I blathered on, the words uncharacteristically flowing from my mouth. I certainly had not prepared to give a speech. It was almost like some outside force was trying to give me the right words. I worked myself into such a dither that tears were starting to well up in my eyes.

The Air Force had a policy on dealing with students who busted a checkride. They would get two additional training rides and then take a second checkride which was referred to as the *elimination ride*. If the student busted that checkride, they were out.

Lt. Tracy politely listened without interrupting and added a few comforting words at the end.

"Do not give up, George. Let me see what I can do to help. I will schedule us to fly tomorrow and we will see if we can figure out what went wrong."

He knew my piloting abilities. He had been my instructor for all the lessons leading up to the checkride. He knew that I could fly the airplane or he would not have put me up for the checkride in the first place.

When I returned home that night, it was not hard for Sandy to tell from the pitiable look on my face that something had gone terribly wrong. That first checkride in the T-37 program was the most critical one. The washout rate from busting it was high. It was during this checkride that students often cracked under pressure. The retake would be even more stressful.

The next day, word quickly spread throughout the class that I had busted the checkride. I detected snickering and whispering behind my back, especially from a somewhat pompous classmate.

"I knew he was not going to make it."

He made me feel even worse when he came up to me with his chest puffed out.

"When you bust the next checkride, you can always go to navigator training."

To him, it was not a matter of *if*, but *when*. As a navigator, I would still be considered an aviator; I just would not be a pilot. It got me thinking about my options if I busted out, and it was not where my mind needed to be at that critical time.

A good instructor wanted to see his students succeed in pilot training. When one of his students washed out, it was somewhat of a negative reflection on him. Maybe he was not teaching the correct technique; maybe he was putting students up for checkrides when they were not ready; maybe his teaching techniques were not good, or he was not getting the procedures across to the student. The T-37 instructor position was not the most highly sought-after job in the Air Force. For some instructors, their class standing when they graduated from pilot training was not high enough to get a desirable assignment to fly fighters, bombers, or transport aircraft. Thankfully, my instructor was a mild-mannered individual who wanted to be an instructor and seemed to enjoy teaching students. He made me feel comfortable in my association with him.

The primary emphasis on my two additional training flights was on the two maneuvers that I had screwed up on the checkride: the spin recovery and the engine out approach and landing. I had not been aggressive enough in pushing the stick forward during the spin recovery. At home, I created a crude simulator using a cardboard box for the instrument panel and a broom for the control stick. I practiced the maneuver over, and over, and over again, applying the full opposite rudder, then abruptly moving that stick forward. I practiced this procedure with such intensity that I broke the broomstick.

I desperately needed help so at night I prayed, probably more emphatically than I ever had prayed in my life. It was more than just *Now I lay me down to sleep*, or the *Lord's Prayer*.

My prayers were probably not very saintly in content, if that is the correct term, but hopefully the message got across to the one that mattered.

Lord, I am asking for your help to pass this checkride. You brought me this far, please, please do not let me fail now.

When Sandy was not around, I even got down on my knees beside the bed, looked up to the ceiling with my hands folded and prayed like it was coming from my heart. This was a critical time for me. Who better to rely on for help than the Lord? But would he come through for me?

I believed that I could pass the checkride, but I had to prove it to a check airman. I mentioned to my instructor that I felt intimidated by the previous check airman's stern mannerisms. It made me nervous to have someone just sitting there watching my every move, writing stuff, and not saying anything. My instructor told me that there was an unwritten protocol that students were permitted to request some personal interaction from the evaluator provided it did not interfere with the conduct of the checkride. Obviously, a check airman was not going to carry on a conversation about family in the middle of a spin recovery. However, when he greeted me or when we were walking to the airplane, he could be cordial to help put me at ease.

My day of reckoning came with a pleasant surprise. Most likely it was prearranged by my instructor, or possibly it was the result of input from a higher entity—maybe both. The check airman for my checkride would be the squadron commander who was a low key, gentlemanly type of person, someone with whom I could feel comfortable. His office was adjacent to our training room, so I did not have to make that lonely trek to the dreaded building where the check airmen operated. For the checkride, I only needed to repeat the maneuvers that I had previously failed. I still had to fly the airplane to the training area, so any screw-ups along the way would count against me. I did the required maneuvers and then the major took over flying the airplane. I initially thought that I had done something wrong, but it just meant that the major wanted to get some stick time. All I had to do was sit back, watch, and breathe a sigh of relief. I could now move on to the next phase of T-37 training.

ACADEMICS

There were several ground school courses covering many different subjects. The courses were conducted nearly every weekday, and practical training was done in conjunction with some of the courses.

The ejection seat and parachute in an aircraft were designed to propel a pilot's body clear of an unflyable aircraft and then safely return him to earth. The sequence was activated by the pilot pulling the ejection seat handles. Small charges blew the canopy clear of the aircraft, and within milliseconds, the seat was rocketed upward more than 100 feet. A charge was automatically activated to discard the seat. The pilot would then free fall to a preset altitude, at which time the parachute opened. The ejection sequence was engineered to perfection and was probably one of the most complex systems on the aircraft. Just in case it did not work as advertised, students were instructed on how to manually separate from the seat, how to manually deploy the parachute, and how to deploy the emergency parachute if all else failed. God forbid any of this would happen to me, but it was good to know just in case.

Along with ejection seat academics, students were given practical training in an ejection seat simulator located inside the tallest building on base. Each trainee took a turn in the simulator. When the ejection handles were squeezed, a simulated detonation of an explosive charge under the pilot's seat activated a 7 G kick in the rear end. The force of gravity that keeps humans from floating off the earth is 1 G, so 7 Gs exert seven times that amount of force, which causes a sudden and severe jolt to the body. To prevent neck injury, students were emphatically instructed to keep their heads back against the headrest.

The seat was rocketed upward along a long metal rail. One of the jokesters in the class said he hoped there was a pin at the top of the rail to stop the seat from going through the roof. Most everybody laughed, except the instructors, who had probably heard it several times.

The ejection training took a toll on my whiplashed neck injury. The jolt caused it to flame up again, so I had a very sore neck for several days afterwards. But there could be no complaining, and certainly no visit to the flight surgeon. I just had to endure it.

Next up was parasail training. Trainees were transported by bus to an open grass field on the base. A long rope was wrapped around a winch attached to the bed of a pickup truck. Students were given instructions on how to land after coming down in a parachute and execute a PLF (parachute landing fall). The important points to remember were to:

1. Keep legs slightly bent at the knees.
2. Chin and elbows tucked in.
3. Keep the feet together.
4. Once on land, collapse onto the ground and release from the parachute.

Those sounded like straightforward instructions. Students were fitted with a harness that surrounded their chest. The long rope from the truck winch was attached to a D-ring sewn into the harness near the center of the student's chest. Attached to the rear of the student's harness was a parachute. The student, truck, and parachute were then oriented into the wind. Two instructors grabbed the edges of the parachute and flipped it open so that the wind started inflating it. When it was partially inflated, students were commanded to start running—then to run faster and faster.

The truck and the speedy student simultaneously moved forward as the rope tugged and pulled on the student. Within a few steps, the parachute was fully inflated, and the student was airborne. He was towed until the rope on the truck was nearly vertical in the air. Using a megaphone, the instructor issued commands.

"Release the rope."

The student pushed a lever to open the D-ring and the rope fell to the ground. The student was now floating back to the ground under the parachute.

The instructor emphatically issued a series of commands: "Keep your chin tucked in," he barked. "Elbows together." As the student drifted closer to the ground, he reminded him, "Feet together." He increased his emphasis, "Feet together!" Finally, the instructor was almost shouting into the megaphone as one student neared the ground. "*Feet together!*" For that classmate, the instructor did not mince words as he bellowed into the megaphone. "*Get your damned feet together!*"

The student either was not listening, or he thought that he did not need to respect the commands of the enlisted instructor. It was emphasized during the briefing that landing with feet apart was a sure way to break a leg. That is what he did, and sure enough, that is what happened. A flight surgeon and ambulance were present, and the training came to a stop while the student was strapped to a gurney and transported to the base hospital. Another classmate broke his leg within a one-hour time-period, so my class size quickly decreased by two.

Physiology ground school was accompanied by a practical training session in a hypobaric chamber, or altitude chamber, as it was commonly called. The coursework consisted of teaching students the negative effects of flight on the human body. The emphasis was on hypoxia, which could result in disastrous consequences for a pilot.

Because the air at higher altitudes is thinner than the air on the ground, it contains less oxygen. Deprivation of oxygen to the brain causes hypoxia, which can lead to unconsciousness or death. In fighter type aircraft such as the T-37, supplemental oxygen is continuously available to the pilot through the oxygen mask. If the oxygen system fails, the oxygen bottle is depleted, smoke in the cockpit interferes with the body's ability to absorb oxygen, or the pressurization system fails, the lack of oxygen to the body causes the mind to become lethargic and eventually quit functioning. The US Air Force not only loses an airplane but a highly trained pilot in whom they have invested a lot of money.

Low atmospheric pressure at high altitudes prevents the body from absorbing oxygen. For high-flying aircraft, pressurization systems maintain the pressure inside the cockpit to a safe level. The T-37 did not have a pressurization system, so the maximum altitude at which the aircraft could be flown was 25,000 feet. There was a strong emphasis on conducting a thorough preflight check of the oxygen system. It was called the PRICE check, which was a mnemonic for pressure, regulator, indicator, connections, and emergency. The Air Force used a lot of memory joggers as methods for remembering a series of items.

The altitude chamber training was designed so students could experience the effects of hypoxia. It looked like a huge, rectangular insulated box with large vacuum pumps and hoses attached to one end. The pumps sucked ambient air from this airtight container to simulate high altitude conditions. Highly trained Air Force enlisted personnel were in command of the chamber. Trainees were seated inside while the instructors first regulated the environment to an altitude of 10,000 feet. Trainees were instructed to check the function of their oxygen masks and regulators. Then the chamber pressure was increased to simulate the conditions at sea level.

"Did anyone have trouble clearing their ears?" the instructors asked.

A couple of guys raised their hands. Congestion in sinuses could prevent the air pressure in ear canals from equalizing with the outer air pressure. If pilot ear passageways were not cleared, the eardrum could burst. It was better to be honest than to suffer a busted eardrum, which could end your flying career.

"Do a Valsalva. Close your mouth, pinch the end of your nose and blow hard," we were told.

Most times it worked, and the ears popped. Those students who could not clear their ears were pulled out of the chamber and would need to go back another day.

The chamber environment was then taken to an equivalent of 30,000 feet. Trainees were instructed to remove their oxygen masks and wait for their symptoms of hypoxia to appear. Symptoms were unique to each trainee, but common ones included light headedness, dizziness, and skin color change to blue. Instructors in the chamber watched every student closely, in case they became too hypoxic and went unconscious. Without oxygen, time of useful consciousness at 25,000 feet is three to five minutes. It decreases to thirty seconds at 35,000 feet, and nine seconds at 45,000 feet. If a pilot is unconscious, he is unable to don his oxygen mask and would die within a short period of time.

With oxygen masks off at 30,000 feet, trainees were given simple tasks to perform such as writing their names or adding numbers. As the student became hypoxic, the tasks got harder. Students were expected to recognize when they were becoming hypoxic and to don their oxygen mask. The mask-off exercise was not a contest to see who could stay off oxygen the longest, or who had the goofiest symptoms. It was designed so students could learn their symptoms of hypoxia and respond correctly.

Another aviation physiological hazard is vertigo. It occurs when the little hair fibers in the semicircular canal of the ear become confused between sensation versus reality. These little hairs sense the motion of fluid within those canals. Normal gravitational forces on the ground keep the fluid and hairs in a position that corresponds with what we visualize with our eyes. In flight, it is easy to confuse these hairs. An aircraft could be in a forty-five or sixty-degree banked turn, or even be inverted, and still be in a one G condition. If flight is in the clouds, the pilot has no visual references with objects on the ground to determine upright from upside down. The pilot could fly the aircraft into an unsafe attitude if he relied only on inputs from those little hairs.

To simulate vertigo, students were strapped into a Barany chair. They closed their eyes and an instructor spun the chair. After a period of rotating at a constant speed in the chair, the fluid in the ear stabilized and the pilot falsely thought rotation had stopped. The chair was then brought to an abrupt stop. It caused the fluid within the ear to move again. The little hairs sensed movement of the fluid, but the pilot's body was now at a standstill. When the student opened his eyes, the sensations from his eyes conflicted with those from his ears and caused the dizzying condition known as vertigo.

Vertigo has been the scourge for many inadequately trained aviators. To prevent vertigo-related accidents, Air Force pilots were taught to visually rely only on flight instruments in the cockpit, and not on the erroneous sensations from their body. Physiology was a preparatory course for the instrument training phase in the T-37.

Meteorology was another instrument training related course and it was interesting and somewhat easy for me. I had taken meteorology and climatology courses in college. All that stuff about cold and warm fronts, high- and low-pressure systems, isobars and isotherms, cloud types, and thunderstorms were familiar to me. There was still more to learn but I had a head start. Some classmates struggled on the written exam; I got a good grade.

Instrument Flight Rule (IFR) ground school was probably the most difficult of all the academic courses. IFR rules were very comprehensive and extensive. The Air Force bible for instrument flying was AFM 51-37. Like the airplane dash one, which was the comprehensive aircraft manual, the instrument flying manual was a very well-known manual just by its numerical designation. It had a lot of terminology in it that was important to know and understand.

Then there were all those symbols on the aviation charts and maps. Each symbol represented a specific feature. A six-sided polygon represented the location of a VOR transmitter; if three sides of that polygon were bold, then it was a combined VOR and TACAN station; if the polygon also had a square box around it, then it was a VOR with DME (distance measuring equipment) capability. There were lines for contours, symbols for obstacles, shading for prohibited areas, plus hundreds more map representations. It was necessary to know the meaning and significance of every depiction on an aviation map.

This vast amount of information caused many students to struggle on the instrument procedures final exam. A couple of guys tried to help each other and got caught. Cheating was absolutely forbidden. It was antithetical to the Air Force policy on integrity. My class size decreased by another two and I was not unhappy to see those two cheaters go, especially since they were trying to better their scores to the detriment of my class standing.

BOUGHT THE FARM

Checkride and academic scores for each student were updated after each major ground school event, and after each checkride. High scores were important for class standing at the end of pilot training because it determined the order in which students would get to select their airplane assignment. To get a fighter jet, you needed to be in the upper echelon of class standing. I was doing good on the academic scores but not so good on checkride scores because of that one T-37 checkride bust.

Instrument flight training in the T-37 involved students flying under a hood to simulate flying in the clouds. The hood was placed over the students helmet such that he could only see the instruments inside the cockpit with no visual references to the outside. The hood was pulled down shortly after takeoff and not raised again until on final approach to landing, when the student had to see the runway to land. The instructor raised the hood at 100 feet above ground if he wanted the student to land. One hundred feet was the minimum altitude to break out of the clouds on approach to landing, see the runway, and still land. If the student did not see the runway at 100 feet, he was expected to go around. To develop the student's decision-making ability, sometimes the instructor would raise the hood at 100 feet and sometimes he would not. The student needed to make the correct decision.

After instrument training, it was on to some flying that was more fun to learn. In formation flying, we switched back and forth between flying as lead or flying as a wingman. The formation maneuvers were much the same as in the initial phase of T-37 training, with loops, rolls, lazy eights, and so forth— except that now the flying was done in a formation of two aircraft. Lead was expected to lead and wingmen were expected to follow. Flying as a wingman in a two-ship formation entailed flying just a few feet off the wingtip of lead. If lead did a barrel roll, the wingman did a barrel roll right along with lead. Lead needed to be smooth so his wingman could stay in position. A wingman needed to be intensely focused on lead's airplane and have total confidence in the lead pilot's ability to safely guide the flight.

There was a weekly briefing to the class by one of the instructors. It consisted of notifying students of changes to their dash one, checklist, and AFM 51-37. The currency of each student's manual was inspected on checkrides.

The Air Force placed a considerable emphasis on safety, so the briefing also included safety-related topics. The human is the fallible component of the man-machine element in aviation, so this part of the briefing focused on learning from other pilot's mistakes. One day the safety briefing had an especially somber tone.

"There was a T-37 accident yesterday. It involved a student and his instructor from another squadron on this base. They were practicing spins and were unable to recover. Their bodies were found near the wreckage. An aircraft accident investigation board has been appointed by the general in charge of Air Training Command. They will evaluate all the possible causes and will release their findings within thirty days. Preliminary findings based on reports from another pilot in the area indicate that the aircraft was possibly in a flat spin."

A flat spin was different from an oscillating nose up, nose down, yawing, and rolling type of spin from which we were trained to recover. In a flat spin, the aircraft was spinning around an imaginary vertical axis like a flat saucer, as it plummeted to the ground. During spin training, an aircraft could inadvertently enter a flat spin, and standard spin recovery procedures may or may not work to recover the aircraft.

"If I were to speculate on the cause," he said, "I would think that the student most likely had attempted the standard spin recovery procedure. The aircraft probably did not come out of the spin. The instructor then took over, but he could not get the aircraft out of the spin either. It appeared that they stayed with the airplane too long."

Meaning they did not eject prior to the minimum altitude of 10,000 feet. A pilot's tendency was to try everything possible to prevent losing an airplane. It was mentally difficult to decide to eject his body from the confines of an aircraft cockpit into a 250 mile per hour blast of air.

"When they finally ejected, there was not enough altitude for their parachutes to open. The lesson to be learned here is that it is critical that pilots eject from an uncontrollable aircraft before the minimum altitude of 10,000 feet. Do not press below that altitude attempting to save the aircraft. Aircraft are replaceable, you are not."

When Air Force aviators got killed in an aircraft accident, pilots facetiously tried to minimize the nature of the situation. Some might call it gallows humor. We referred to it as *buying the farm*.

Most people were buried in a grave. Graves were typically two and one-half feet wide, six feet long, and six feet deep. That plot of land in pilot parlance was referred to as *the farm*. When a pilot was killed, he bought the farm.

Most likely, every student in the class was now going through some type of self-examination about why they were doing this. Flying jets in the Air Force was a hazardous occupation. Even insurance companies had higher rates for life insurance policies on pilots. Accidents and death were part of flying fighter jets. People died in this business.

The accident investigation board would look at possible mechanical malfunctions. Like any man-made machine, components on an aircraft occasionally failed. To alleviate this from happening, detailed records were kept on each component in an aircraft and parts were replaced when they neared the end of their useful life. It was not a fail-safe process.

Every Air Force aircraft had an enlisted crew chief assigned to it. It was their *baby*, and from an appearance and mechanical standpoint, their aircraft was kept in immaculate condition. The crew chief had a cadre of systems specialists at his beckoning to diagnose and fix problems on his aircraft if they arose. If an attitude indicator failed, the crew chief called in a specialist from avionics; if a fuel pump failed, he called in one from fuels; if an engine failed, he called in someone from propulsion.

Like pilots, Air Force mechanics were extensively trained to follow exacting procedures. At the end of performing a maintenance procedure, each mechanic was required to account for every tool they used to do the maintenance. That policy resulted from the findings of an accident that occurred several years prior. The investigators found that a set of mechanic's pliers left behind in an airplane throttle quadrant had wiggled into a position during flight to jam the throttles into the idle position. It was an isolated incident that was not representative of the professionalism of mechanics who did a great job of maintaining our airplanes. Air Force mechanics were highly respected by pilots and were referred to as the *best of the best*.

I earned increasing respect from my instructor for my potential to be an Air Force pilot. I loved formation flying and was exceptionally proficient at it. My instructor sometimes took control of the aircraft because he said that I did not need all the stick time.

Class size stabilized at fifty-four and washouts were down to zero. Rumor had it, and perhaps there was some validity to it, that by this stage of training, the Air Force had invested a considerable amount of money in training a student and they wanted to keep you. True or not, the rumor made me feel good. It was a confidence builder that I was probably going to make it through pilot training, barring any unforeseen screwups.

COCKY

T he next stage of pilot training was the T-38 phase. The T-38 was a sleek-looking, twin-engine jet aircraft. Its long, white, slightly humpbacked fuselage and swept back wings would have created an even more streamlined aircraft if the pilot cockpits did not necessitate a slight bulge on the top of the fuselage. The pointed nose made me fantasize that some adventurous entrepreneur could miniaturize it into a flying pencil. It had all the appearances of a true fighter jet. Students wore a patch on their flight suit that depicted the outline of a T-38. The Air Force crack demonstration team, the Thunderbirds, flew the T-38. It was okay for T-38 students to be a little cocky.

The T-38 aircraft was designed to withstand high G-forces up to 7.33 Gs. That was 7.33 times the pull of gravity on the earth. It was important to moderate the effects of these high G-forces on a pilot's body. At 4 Gs, the pilot starts to lose his vision. Blood drains from the pilot's head into his lower extremities. With increasing G forces, the pilot loses consciousness.

Because of its high G capability, T-38 pilots wore a G suit that made them look like a *macho* fighter pilot. The G suit was zipped up around the pilot's waist and legs. It was plugged into a receptacle in the airplane. As G forces increased, sensors inside the airplane activated airflow to the G suit that squeezed the pilot's legs and waist. It prevented blood from draining from the upper extremities of the pilot's body, and especially from the brain. As soon as the stick was released and the G forces subsided, the G suit deflated. In a dogfight with an enemy aircraft, the ability to pull high Gs gave the pilot a definite advantage over an enemy.

A combat version of the T-38, the F-5 Freedom Fighter, was a single-seat military combat fighter jet. It could be loaded with 6,200 pounds of ordnance, a 20mm canon, and four air-to-air missiles. The T-38 was nicknamed the *Talon*, like the claw for a bird of prey. The name Talon just did not fit the description for the T-38. It was hard to imagine how a sleek-looking fighter jet looked like the claw of a bird. If somebody asked about flying the Talon, it likely elicited a look of bewilderment.

The T-38 had tandem seating, meaning there were front and rear cockpits. When practicing flight maneuvers like loops or barrel rolls, or when flying in formation, the student sat in the front cockpit. For instrument flying, the student sat in the rear cockpit with a curtain pulled underneath the canopy. Compared to the claustrophobia-inducing helmet hood used in the T-37, it was a comfortable improvement. With the curtain, at least the student could see the entire inside of the cockpit; he just could not see outside the cockpit. If a student wanted to cheat, he could leave it cracked open to see outside, but I did not want to get caught if the instructor checked, so I never did it.

We flew standard confidence-building maneuvers in the T-38, such as loops, rolls, and lazy eights. Formation flying consisted of two-ship and four-ship formations. One syllabus requirement was to fly a weekend cross country trip. I was proud of the T-38 and wanted to show it off to my hometown folks by flying over Ma and Dad's house. I convinced my instructor that my hometown was a nice place to visit. We could visit Dad's favorite hangouts, imbibe some adult beverages, and then recover at Ma and Dad's house. I enthusiastically planned the cross-country flight and even plotted the location of Ma and Dad's house on a topographic map so that we could easily locate it from the air.

The day before we were to leave, the weather forecast turned bad, with possible icing conditions along our route. The T-38 could not be flown through icing conditions, so I had to plan my cross country to another base.

That weather potentially saved my flying career in another way. We later learned that an Air Force fighter pilot had previously done a flyby over his home town, but he did a little more than just fly over it. He tried to put on an airshow. He got a little too aggressive, tried to perform a roll at low altitude and crashed. The higher-ups in the Air Force thereafter frowned on unauthorized flyovers and considered anyone who did it as demonstrating poor judgement. Had my instructor and I done my hometown flyover and gotten caught, they probably would have taken away my instructor's wings and washed me out of pilot training. The icing conditions could not have materialized at a more opportune time.

All fifty-four of us remaining in the class made it through the T-38 phase of pilot training. I could not believe that I had done it. This daredevil farm kid, high school screw-off, and studiously challenged college student had made it through Air Force pilot training to earn the highly coveted wings of an Air Force pilot.

In addition to Sandy and Paul, I invited Ma and Dad, Eunice and her husband, Gene, to my graduation. I showed them around the base and let them sit inside a T-38. Ma and Dad were extremely proud of their son. They could go back home and express their pride in me to the hometown folks. Nobody back home had ever been a fighter pilot.

The graduation ceremony was a formal military mess dress occasion. The mess dress was the military equivalent of a civilian tuxedo, with custom-fitted trousers, jacket, and cummerbund, white shirt with bow tie, and spit-polished shoes that shined like a mirror. My 2nd Lieutenant rank was emblazoned on a cloth-covered lapel that was slid under holder strips on the coat shoulders. The most honorable awards insignia could be pinned on the left breast but since I had not yet earned any commendations, my chest was absent any medals. Drinks were plentiful, dinner was served, toasts were proclaimed, and everybody was happy. Then it was time to award the coveted Air Force wings to each of the graduates. The wing commander announced:

"Lieutenant George Kohn, please come forward."

I popped out of my chair, smartly stepped forward, snapped a sharp salute to the presenting colonel, and received my wings. I was now officially an Air Force pilot. It was a badge of high honor to now wear the wings of a pilot in the esteemed United States Air Force.

The Air Force Assignments Division posted a list of aircraft available for our future assignment. Graduates selected their preference and were awarded an assignment based on their class standing. The block of aircraft assignments for my class consisted of a mix of airplanes such as the F-100, F-4, T-38, T-37, C-130, C-123, C-47, B-52, and even a couple of UH-1s, even though they were helicopters. I would later learn that there was good reason to respect helicopter pilots as being among the bravest of the brave.

There were limited numbers of assignments to most of the airplanes. The top two graduates took the only two single-seat F-100 fighter jets. In 1969, the war in Vietnam was going strong and the F-4 Phantom fighter jet was a workhorse in the bombing campaign. There was a need for F-4 pilots. I graduated number sixteen in my class and got a backseat F-4 assignment.

PART FOUR

OBJECTIVE PURSUED

My first stop after leaving Texas was to a base in southern Florida for water survival school. I could not swim, and it terrified me that I was going to be dropped into the Atlantic Ocean to practice surviving. Students were transported to the training area on a flat-deck propelled barge. We were strapped into a harness with a parachute attached to it, sort of like the parasail training. A long rope was attached to a winch on a tow boat idling off the rear of the barge. The barge was oriented into the wind to inflate the parachute, a signal was given for the student to start running; and the tow boat took off. I ran toward the end of the barge, dropped off the end of it, ran across the top of the water for a few steps, and then went airborne. On the instructor's command, I released the tow rope and started a slow descent toward the ocean while checking to make sure I knew the exact location of the tabs on my life vest. When my feet hit the water, I released the parachute so that the wind would not blow it across the water with me attached. With a big gasp of air, I held my breath and sank below the surface of the warm ocean water. I pulled the tabs, and the inflated life preserver floated me back to the surface.

In a real ejection, the pilot would deploy a life raft as part of his survival gear. For this training, the instructors towed an inflated raft to each pilot. Students were instructed to connect it to their harness so that it would not float away. It was emphasized to expeditiously get into the raft because there were sharks in the area. US Air Force sharpshooters continuously circled the area in a patrol boat in case any were a threat. Tasks while floating in the raft consisted of simulated repair of a leaky raft, activation of a radio beacon, shooting off flares, checking the first aid kit, and indulging in some of the yummy survival supplies. It was relaxing to bob across the gentle waves in the ocean while basking in the Florida sunshine. All too soon, I had to use a signal mirror to direct a helicopter to pluck me out of the warm ocean water.

Next up was Air Force survival school to learn survival in a hostile environment. It was January and there was three feet of snow on the ground in the eastern part of the state of Washington. It was nearly impossible to walk anywhere without wearing snowshoes. The first exercises simulated a World War II type of POW (prisoner of war) environment. Everyone was captured and directed into mock prisoner of war camps and interrogated. Name, rank, and serial number were all you were supposed to provide, even though they tried to pry additional information out of you through verbal intimidation and threats of physical torture.

The interrogators were enlisted Air Force personnel who spoke with authentic German accents. Some were *good guy* interrogators, and some were *bad guy* interrogators. The good guys offered you a reward if you ratted on your cohorts; the bad guy interrogators threatened you.

"Comrade Kohn, here is a cigarette for you. Now tell me the name of your commander?"

Or, "Comrade Kohn, if you do not cooperate, I can have you shot."

As simulated prisoners, we were encouraged to plot an escape. Escapees were pretend-shot and got to spend the rest of the exercise in a nice warm building. Escapees were usually the higher-ranking officers. I had to remain in prison and huddle around an open wood fire in the prison yard to stay warm.

Information about the treatment of United States war prisoners in Vietnam was filtering back to US intelligence agencies through clandestine channels. I was taught about how to communicate through those channels if the need arose. POWs were enduring brutal physical torture at the hands of the North Vietnamese. With an assignment to the

F-4, it was certain that I was going to Vietnam, so the training scenario at survival school focused on escape, evasion, capture, and survival in a hostile Vietnam scenario. Although instructors were not permitted to use physical force on students, there were other ways to demonstrate the nasty effects of being a North Vietnamese prisoner. They contorted my body to fit into a small wooden box. I was dragged into an isolated prison cell that closely approximated those in the Hanoi Hilton. There was harsh interrogation during which we were expected to comply with the rules of the Geneva convention by giving only name, rank, and serial number. The interrogators wanted more. We were briefed that the pain from beatings by the North Vietnamese interrogators could get so bad that it was okay to make up faulty information, or to play dumb. I carried the dumb part a little too far. During the debriefing after the exercise, it was suggested that my dumb strategy would probably not be convincing with this enemy. The North Vietnamese were smart people. They already knew a lot about the American method of conducting war from reading US media reports. I needed a more convincing approach for dealing with interrogators, should the need arise.

After this, it was on to California to learn the F-4. It was a complex multipurpose aircraft that could drop bombs (conventional or nuclear), intercept and shoot down enemy aircraft in a dogfight, launch rockets, or fire a 20mm (millimeter) gun to attack airborne or ground targets. It had tandem seating, meaning there was a front seater (aircraft commander, or AC) and a back seater (guy in the back, or GIB). Most GIBs were young pilots right out of pilot training, but some were navigators. I was a GIB and it posed some limitations in terms of flying the F-4. GIBs were not in charge of the aircraft; the aircraft commander was in charge. GIBs could not raise and lower the gear; the only gear handle was in the front cockpit. GIBs could not drop bombs; the only bomb release button was in the front. GIBs did not normally take off or land; there was limited visibility forward to see the runway for landing.

Controls for the F-4 navigation system were only in the rear cockpit. It was a very sophisticated system for that era of aviation. The system was based on the principles of a spinning gyroscope. Much like a child's toy, a spinning gyroscope remains erect. Pendulums were attached to this gyroscope that swung in response to motion of the aircraft. The movement of the pendulums were picked up by sensors. Sensor information was sent to a computer that translated it into distance travelled. If the system were programmed with a known starting point, it could then track distances and directions in relation to that starting point. It was called an inertial navigation system (INS) and in 1969 this INS encompassed the latest in navigation technology. It was useful for navigating to and from a target area. When it was accurate, it could be used to locate and bomb a target; if not, bombs could be thrown way off target.

Two student ACs in the F-4 class were prior F-4 GIBs in Europe who were upgrading to the front seat. They were competing to see who could get the best scores in their upgrade training. They also made it known that they were competing to see who could be the first to make it to the rank of General. Scores in training were based on the accuracy of dropping miniature versions of a real 500-pound bomb on a target. During the dive toward the target, GIBs were responsible for calling out altitudes and airspeeds to the AC. Most importantly, GIBs made sure the front seater did not press—that is, descend— below a minimum bomb release altitude. Front seaters were also graded on air to air intercepts, which directly involved the GIB using the backseat radar to acquire and lock on to an airborne target.

One of these two ACs was paired with a tactful GIB who had been in my pilot training class. The other AC got me. My reputation may have preceded me. I did not come across well when first meeting him and I could almost read his mind: *How did I end up with this guy?*

It was obvious that once again, I could not depend on my social skills to make a good impression and would have to prove that I was a capable pilot. After several missions to the bombing range, he may have recognized my conscientious effort to do a good job. His scores were nearly equal to those of his competitive friend with his suave GIB.

FIGHT IN FIGHTER PILOT

Before each training mission, an instructor conducted a briefing on weather, formation procedures, route to and from the range, bombing procedures and techniques, formation rejoin, and return to base. For one training mission the instructor had the appearance of a disgruntled major. He spoke with a gruff voice, his closed lips curved downward, his eyebrows squeezed together, and a wrinkled forehead indicated that he did not want to have any degree of cordiality with his students. He was stuck with flying training missions when he probably wanted an F-4 assignment to Vietnam. Combat experience would look good on his promotion record. His dissatisfaction was expressed by the condescending remarks he made to his students.

"If you cannot get that jink maneuver right, you are going to get your ass shot off in Vietnam."

Training flights were four-ship formations. To minimize congestion in the California skies, we flew a predesignated FAA color-coded route to the bombing range.

This major briefed a blue route, so I raised my hand.

"On a mission last week, we flew the orange route to the range and there was less delay than on a previous mission when we flew on the blue route."

The room got quiet. The only sound was a deep sigh from my AC. How could his lowly lieutenant back seat trainee be so brazen as to question a decision by a highly experienced F-4 aircraft commander instructor?

"Lieutenant, I have been flying this airplane along these routes for a long time. If I need any help with this briefing, I will ask for it. Do you understand?"

I sheepishly responded.

"Yes sir."

My aircraft commander was visibly ashamed of me. His eyes rolled, he looked down and away from me. He was obviously thinking: *Why couldn't this guy keep his mouth shut?*

I felt like crawling under the table. I had just been verbally reprimanded in front of six other pilots for saying something that I thought would be helpful. What was it about me that elicited such disrespect for making, what I thought, was a worthwhile suggestion?

I was not totally disappointed with myself, even though I wished I had never opened my mouth. I wanted to talk to somebody, but I could not gather the courage to do so. Instead, I did some reflection about what I needed to do to succeed in this fighter pilot environment.

In pilot training, there had been a degree of student subservience to instructors. Most students were second lieutenants. Instructors were higher ranking 1st lieutenants and captains. There was decency and respect between instructors and students regardless of rank or position. F-4 training was different in that some students were higher ranking than the instructors. One of the students that day was a lieutenant colonel selectee transitioning from another aircraft into the F-4. He also offered a suggestion during the briefing, but the instructor knew better that to reprimand him. I quickly learned that I was at the bottom of the pecking order and was therefore a magnet for scorn. I did some deep self-analysis.

Yes, this guy was an instructor. Yes, this guy was a major with lots of rank over me. Maybe I was wrong to offer this suggestion, but I did it with good intentions.

I had been raised with an understanding that regardless of position in life, there must be common decency. An Air Force motto was that an officer cannot command respect; he must earn it. This major certainly did not earn any respect from me with his snarky response. I had been taught that it was virtuous to be humble. Maybe it was in catechism class where I learned about Jesus' teaching: *Be completely humble and patient* (Ephesians 4:2). This guy did not have the courtesy to show decency and respect toward me and I was upset about it. Okay, perhaps a better term was that I was *pissed off.* Being a new pilot, maybe this was the spark that I needed to instill some *fight* in me to survive in the demanding fighter pilot environment.

It was customary that each AC invited their GIB to their house for drinks and dinner. Sandy and I looked forward to it. Sandy was well-spoken and likable. She could carry on an interesting conversation with anybody in a social setting. She was a blessing for me, because I could let her do most of the talking while I sat quietly and listened. Maybe I could get some respect for my choice of her as my wife.

My AC's wife was sort of attractive, small-in-stature, prim, and proper. It was likely that her husband had already talked to her about me. She acted somewhat like she assumed the rank of her captain husband when she commanded Sandy and I to take our assigned seats. It started out as a nice evening. She prepared a delicious dinner for us and we had some drinks. The conversation was cordial. After dinner, I had to pee. I politely asked to use their bathroom, went in, did my thing, and returned to the living room. A short time later, she went into the bathroom and came out in a fury.

"Somebody peed on the toilet seat."

My mind was racing with thoughts about her comment, which was clearly directed at me. I thought I knew the proper graces for using someone's toilet. Then again, I did grow up on a farm that only had an outdoor toilet which I never used. If I had to go, I just whipped it out next to a tractor tire or by the corner of a farm building and let 'er rip. There was no need to be precise with the aim.

So how did pee end up on her toilet seat? Maybe all the drinks caused me to forget to raise the seat. Or, maybe her husband piddled on the seat before I even went to the toilet. The *somebody peed on my toilet seat* comment caused all conversation to suddenly stop. Since her comment was obviously directed at me, I felt shame. I could not wait to finish my drink and get the heck out of there. I did not deserve to be this magnet for disrespect and scorn, especially considering what was in the offing for me.

Everyone in F-4 training knew they were going to Southeast Asia, where the life of a fighter pilot in combat would reveal its ugliness. The Vietnam War was going strong in 1969 and I was on an assignment path that was referred to as *pipeline to Southeast Asia*. Base assignments were scattered throughout Vietnam and Thailand. Thailand was preferred because no war was going on inside Thailand. However, missions were flown out of Thailand into Laos and North Vietnam to support the war in Vietnam. I was assigned to Danang Air Base, Vietnam—in the heart of the war zone—where I would become a member of the famed 366th TFW (Tactical Fighter Wing) known as the Gunfighters.

Before leaving for Vietnam, I got to spend some time at home with Sandy, Paul, Ma, and Dad. Sandy graciously arranged a party at a local dinner club and invited a gathering of friends and relatives. It was time to say goodbye. In the past, I had never exchanged words of emotion or had much physical contact with Ma and Dad. Simple facial expressions and loving gestures usually revealed our feelings toward one another. This was a unique time. Dad had a very somber look on his face as he clasped my hand with both of his hands. Ma and I both had the urge to warmly embrace each other. With tears rolling down her face, she whispered in my ear.

"Please come back to us."

My best friend drove Sandy and me to the airport. I did not wish to spend a lot of time with goodbyes. A quick handshake with John, a hug and kiss on the cheek for Sandy, and I turned, walked away, and did not look back. Fighter pilots were supposed to be macho and not show sad emotions.

PART FIVE

JUNGLE SURVIVAL
STOPOVER

The first segment of the trip to Danang was a civilian flight to San Francisco, where I connected to a military chartered DC-8 airliner full of military personnel heading to Vietnam. The thought crossed my mind that for some on that airplane, it might be a one-way trip. Fighter pilots all deplaned at a stopover at Clark AB in the Philippines to attend a jungle survival school. It was tailored toward surviving in the Southeast Asian jungle environment if we had to punch out of our aircraft. After a brief ground school on jungle edibles, reptiles, and poisonous plants, students were transported into the Philippine jungle to practice evasion.

The terrain had a lot of steep cliffs, but the dense jungle foliage would probably ensnare a person before falling too far. Native inhabitants were a tribe of pygmy people call Negritos. They stood about one-half the height of Americans. They wore only loin cloths, and the women had fully exposed, large, sagging breasts that nearly hung down to their waists. The Negritos moved through the dense jungle foliage swinging razor sharp bolo knives to clear away any obstructions. The US Air Force made a deal with them to help train pilots. They spoke no English and expressed friendliness to American visitors through their gestures. Pilots were expected to evade the Negritos and find a good hiding spot. I thought that I found a good spot but shortly after bedding down for the evening, I got a tap on my shoulder.

"Chit, chit."

The Negritos knew every nook and cranny in that jungle and found every pilot. I had to give the Negrito who found me a chit which he redeemed for a bag of rice, supplied by the US Air Force. It was a fun training exercise that probably saved the lives of many American pilots who were shot down in the hostile Laotian jungle environment.

ON TO DANANG

It was November 1969, and the Vietnam War was increasing in scope and intensity. Danang, Vietnam was located about 180 kilometers (111 miles) south of the DMZ (Demilitarized Zone). The DMZ was a hotbed of combat activity because it was an area that connected the enemy territory in North Vietnam with South Vietnam. The enemy transported war supplies into South Vietnam across that DMZ.

I arrived at Danang with a duffle bag full of military flight suits, underwear, and a few personal photos and toiletries. An *old head* GIB escorted me around the base. I had to sit for newcomer briefings about pay, benefits, insurance, next of kin, and so forth, but the briefings were short compared to those back in the States when I initially entered the Air Force.

The air was permeated with unpleasant odors that had no similarity to the aromas that I grew up smelling on the farm. Even the offensive eye-burning ammonia that emanated from pig manure was no match for stomach churning odors that wafted through the air at Danang. A rotting stench came from bamboo huts inhabited by Vietnamese civilians in Dog Patch village bordering the southwest perimeter of the base. Fermenting fish used in nuoc mam cooking sauce intermingled with the odors of burning rice husks from their cookstoves. Mixed in with this was the putrid smell of decomposing jungle plant material, the American induced odors of JP-4 jet fuel, and the sickeningly sweet smell of the Agent Orange herbicide that US Air Force aircraft sprayed on the countryside to kill vegetation.

The old head GIB drove me to the squadron building to meet the guys, then escorted me to my room in the barracks. I hung a calendar on the closet door to begin the 365-day countdown to DEROS (date estimated return from overseas). Every F-4 pilot in Vietnam knew exactly how many days they had left until DEROS. There were some like me who were in the triple digits, those who had the *double-digit fidgets*, and the lucky ones who were short-timers and going home soon.

Air Force F-4 pilots were provided reasonably good living accommodations, if there was such a thing in a war zone. We flew a three million-dollar asset, so the Air Force wanted us to be well-rested. My room was on the first floor of a two-story modular style barracks. There were two persons per room. A large closet was positioned between the two beds to provide privacy. There was a window above my bed, but I taped a dark blanket over it so I could sleep during the day when I was scheduled for night missions.

Elderly Vietnamese ladies provided maid service if a pilot paid for it. They cleaned the rooms and washed flight suits and underwear for minimal charge. They all wore the traditional baggy black cotton pajamas with loose white shirts and sandals. Outdoors, they wore conical straw hats for protection from the intense tropical sunlight. They spoke limited English but understood numbers one to ten. If a maid liked you that day, you were number one; if not, you were number ten. Not all maids were trustworthy. One was caught trying to carry off an F-4 dash one from a pilot's room. She was fired, but we wondered what a maid was going to do with an F-4 flight manual. We speculated that some were maids during the day and then enemy sympathizers at night. The maids came across as being friendly, but I sensed an indifference or even hostility toward Americans. They probably viewed the Americans as there to bomb their country and kill their people.

Raised platform guard shacks were positioned around the perimeter of the base inside a fence topped with razor wire. They were manned continuously by military police armed with high powered machine guns. The area outside of the fence was infested with suspected VC (Viet Cong).

I could hear the occasional rapid discharge of machine gun fire. Maybe the guards were just clearing their weapons.

The perimeter was defoliated with Agent Orange herbicide sprayed by C-123 Operation Ranch Hand aircraft. It helped the security police to spot suspicious activity. Hardy tropical vegetation grew back quickly, so the C-123s were continually spraying their synthetic herbicide. Those dripping C-123 propeller-driven airplanes were parked next to our F-4s on the flight line so I had to smell and taste that crap. At night, AC 47 Spooky aircraft, and AC 130 Spectre gunship aircraft armed with mini guns, canons, and howitzers, continuously circled the base. They dropped flares to illuminate the area and hosed down any suspicious activity.

ROCKET CITY

Shortly after arriving at Danang, I was awakened one night to a loud whistling sound, a thud, and a jolt that nearly threw me out of bed. Danang was being rocketed. I had been briefed to expect rocket attacks, so I did what I was briefed to do. I donned my pith helmet and crawled under the bed. I did that on the first attack. On subsequent rocket attacks, I did what most of the other pilots did: I went outside to watch the show. The flight path of the rockets was traceable by following their whistling sounds as they approached the base. The rockets had no guidance system, so they hit wherever they were pointed. If my barracks were the target, there was not much I could do about it.

The Air Force had three squadrons of F-4 aircraft at Danang. There were several other aircraft based there that included gunships and rescue helicopters like the HH-3 Sikorsky Jolly Green Giant. A heavy lift Sikorsky Skycrane was occasionally visible in the sky with a damaged aircraft slung under its belly. The Marines had a contingent of F-4s at Danang, and the Army occupied a helicopter and equipment assembly area. The VC could launch unguided rockets anywhere into the base and probably hit something of significance.

Danang AB was nicknamed *rocket city* because of the frequent rocket attacks. There were often fifty or more rockets launched in one attack. Some caused considerable damage to structures on base, some landed in the Dogpatch village just outside the base, probably killing Vietnamese civilians, and some fell harmlessly into open areas near the runway, creating big pockmarks in the landscape.

The squadron operations building was located a short walking distance from the barracks, the 366th Tactical Fighter Wing Headquarters building was just a few steps in another direction, and the flight line was a couple hundred feet from the wing headquarters building. The officers club, hospital, chapel, and dining hall were too far for walking so each squadron had a step van available for anyone's use. It was known as the *bread truck* and it had our squadron emblem emblazoned on the side. If the step van was in use and you wanted to get somewhere, you hitchhiked or hopped on a bus that regularly circled inside the base. Hitchhiking almost always worked. It usually did not take long for somebody to pick you up and maybe even go out of their way to take you wherever you wanted to go.

Meals were served in the dining hall, but I never had much of an appetite. Usually it was most convenient to just get a boxed MRE (meal ready to eat). There were a variety of MREs that had main courses such as beef, spaghetti, ham, or tuna. Each included a side dish, dessert or snack, cheese spread, peanut butter, powdered beverage mix, and seasonings. Most were good, but the tuna was a favorite. In college, we used to joke that you never got sick of eating tuna.

Some industrious pilots found an unused container building, scrounged up some building materials and found a couple of volunteers to build an officer club annex near our three squadron operations buildings. Hamburgers and hotdogs were the main entrees. After eating hamburgers almost every day, I started to gag at the sight of them.

Pilots needed to have a place to unwind after the missions, so our squadron operations building had a refrigerator fully stocked with beer. If you took a beer, it was on the honor system that you paid for it. IOUs were acceptable. Playing darts was a favorite pastime, and there were card games and some gambling, but nothing high stakes. There was a close camaraderie among most of us. We had fun teasing each other about the number of days that each had till DEROS. It did not matter if you were an AC or a GIB, a lieutenant colonel or a lieutenant, it was first name basis for everybody. We were all in this to survive and get back home to *mama*, as our wives were affectionately called.

Squadron ops had a large scheduling board on the wall where pilots were assigned to missions and briefing times were posted. Mission briefings were conducted in the wing headquarters building because it was the only building that was secure for the secret briefings. Pilots had to be careful not to accidently take secret information from those briefings and leave it unattended in the barracks where the maids could steal it.

MISSION TO TCHEPONE

A typical mission to Laos (if there was such a thing) went something like this. Prior to the scheduled show time in wing headquarters, preparation for the mission started in the squadron building. A life support room contained our personal lockers and life support equipment. Enlisted personnel were responsible for cleaning and maintaining our helmets and oxygen masks. Helmets were custom fitted. An unnecessary distraction from a *hot spot* on your head was not something a pilot needed in the heat of battle. Helmets were painted in camouflage green and brown colors. Flight suits were made of gray Nomex fire retardant material. Patches of the wing and squadron emblems were Velcro attached to the flight suit. They had to be removed and stored in your locker prior to a mission so that the enemy could not identify your unit if you were captured. Personal items such as a wallet and pictures of loved ones were left in the locker. Otherwise they could be used to bribe a pilot for information if he were captured. We were required to wear metal dog tags on a chain around our neck. Metal dog tags were engraved with your name, rank, and serial number to assist mortuary personnel with identifying human remains.

We were issued a survival vest that contained one of the most important survival items a pilot could carry—a hand-held VHF (very high frequency) two-way radio. The vest also had pockets that held a signaling mirror, water container, snack items, compass, knife, fire starter, and medical kit. On our waist, we strapped on a holster into which we inserted our .38 caliber pistol. One pilot had a predetermined use for the pistol and loaded his ammo belt full of ammo as though he was going to have a Wild West-style shoot-out with the enemy. If he got shot down and the bad guys were about to get to him, he would at least have the satisfaction of taking some of them out before they got to him. I was unsure what I would use the .38 for until I started hearing stories about the enemy treatment of captured pilots. I had a thought that maybe it would be most effective to use it on myself. Every F-4 pilot also wore a G suit. We would be pulling a lot of Gs to evade the North Vietnamese anti-aircraft missiles and gunfire.

An hour prior to scheduled briefing time, I proceeded to wing headquarters to do target study. Intelligence personnel had prepared a mission folder on the target. We jotted down notes for the mission on six by nine-inch mission reference cards. I wrote the latitude and longitude of the target so that I could insert those numbers into the F-4 inertial navigation system and get guidance to the target. My AC and I reviewed topographic maps of the area so we could visually locate the target in the rugged jungle terrain. A three-dimensional view of the target could be created by placing two of the same topographic maps side by side and using a viewer much like the stereoscope I had as a kid. Intel provided us with known enemy antiaircraft activity in the area so we could plan a run-in to the target that lessened our chances of taking a hit.

The briefings started exactly on time to the second.

"On my hack, the time will be oh eight hundred. Ready, ready, hack."

Military clocks were set to Zulu time, which was the time at zero degrees longitude coinciding with the location of Greenwich, England. Since our area of operation was in one time zone, we all set our watches to local time. Vietnam was twelve hours ahead of the central time zone back home.

The meteorologist started the briefings. Weather could change quickly in Southeast Asia from clear skies and calm winds, to thunderstorms and monsoon conditions. For this mission, weather was not a factor.

Next up was the classified intelligence briefing. There was a secret war taking place in Laos, although it was not very well kept. Already in

1965, our bombings were well known and were covered in the press. From a book titled *Secret War* by Billy G. Webb, "One congressman told reporters the US was bombing the Ho Chi Minh Trail and engaging the communists on the ground in Laos. *The New York Times* even published an article indicating that bombing of the Trail would increase."

During the intelligence briefing we would learn about the plan for our mission.

"The target for today's mission is a suspected truck assembly area on the northern part of the Ho Chi Minh trail in Laos. It is situated in a valley about twenty kilometers southwest of Tchepone. Terrain on both the northwest and southeast sides of the target is mountainous. Since it is near the border with North Vietnam, you must plan your run-in so that you break off before reaching the North Vietnamese border. You will be in proximity to the big guns in North Vietnam; there are known eighty-five millimeter guns two clicks east of your target; and a hundred millimeter gun five clicks to the northeast. SAM sites are also located just across the border in North Vietnam. Since this is a key transit area for the NVA, expect heavy gunfire from the smaller twenty-three, thirty-seven, and fifty-seven millimeter guns. If you take a hit, best egress is to the northwest. There is a CIA safe area about five minutes flying time from your target, so use care not to jettison any ordnance over that area. You should have it marked on your maps. If your airplane is controllable, head west toward Thailand prior to ejecting. Search and rescue will be standing by."

I knew that my mission to Laos would be challenging. The 85mm and 100mm guns were large radar-guided anti-aircraft guns. The NVA (North Vietnamese Army) enemy used radar to track and lock on to your aircraft so that they could precisely direct their gunfire at you. SAMs were surface to air radar-guided missiles. On a SAM launch, enemy radar data is fed into the SAM missile after it is launched. The missile acquires, tracks, closes, and explodes when it impacts your aircraft.

I had been well trained in California on how to deal with those threats. The gun nomenclature referred to the caliber of the gun which, from a pilot standpoint, indicated how fast and how far the gun could shoot. The 23mm, 37mm, and 57mm guns were manually aimed. A North Vietnamese gunner sat on a seat behind twin gun barrels with a sight in front of him. The gun mechanism pivoted on a swivel so that he could turn the gun in any direction and raise and lower the barrel to direct the gunfire at his target. There were numerous 23mm twin-barreled anti-aircraft artillery (AAA) guns throughout Laos. They were small and movable so the locations of AAA sites from our briefing may or may not be accurate. What was important was that there were a lot of them.

My mission for this day consisted of a two-ship formation with each aircraft loaded with eighteen Mark 82 bombs. Each bomb had 500 pounds of explosives, enough to obliterate everything within 200 yards of impact.

Next up was a safety briefing. It was good to occasionally review F-4 bold face procedures. This was not a question and answer session, just a briefing to refresh our memory.

"The memory item for today is ejection. Here is the procedure.

1. Alert other crewmember.
2. Assume proper position.
3. Ejection handle—pull."

The first step in the procedure was important because the tandem seating in the F-4 necessitated that the first to eject was the back seater. If the front seater initiated the ejection sequence, then the back seater was ejected whether he pulled the handles or not. The front seater needed to alert the back seater so that he was in the correct body position with his head back against the head rest. If he were out of position, an ejection could damage or break his neck. The back seater ejected before the front seater so that the flames from the front seater's ejection seat rocket would not burn the back seater as it went up the rail.

If the back seater initiated the ejection, then only the back seater ejected, and the front seater had to initiate his own ejection. There was an exception. The back seater had a handle that he could turn which would sequence the ejection the same as if the front seater initiated the ejection.

This option was available so that the GIB could save an incapacitated front seater.

The lead AC's briefing was next. He was a captain who had several missions under his belt. He followed a checklist to ensure that he covered all the required briefing items. I would be flying with him.

"Gentlemen, takeoff time is ten hundred. We will start engines thirty minutes prior at oh nine thirty. Check in on ground control. We are scheduled to refuel from a tanker on the green track. After dropping off the tanker, we will switch over to ABCCC frequency for clearance into the target area. Remember to complete the combat entry checklist prior to entering the combat area. Our initial orbit altitude will be 15,000 feet. We will be working with a Covey forward air controller today. Call out when you spot him. Lead will be the first in on the target. We will plan on three passes. I will plan on a run-in heading of three one zero degrees but two should offset from that heading to avoid following the same flight track. Target elevation is 1,200 feet. Pickle altitude is 6,200 ft. Do not press. GIBs, make sure you stay on top of this. Pull off is to the west. Jink, jink, jink. Keep your heads on a swivel. Call out RHAW gear warnings, artillery fire or SAM launches on the radio. If you take a hit, try to get as much altitude as possible, broadcast on guard, and switch transponder to emergency setting of 7700. Bingo fuel is 7,000 pounds. Okay? Any questions? See you back here for the debriefing."

Tchepone was a small village in one of the few traversable valleys that provided the NVA access from North Vietnam to the Ho Chi Minh trail in Laos. The trail was the route that the North Vietnamese used to shuttle their armament and wartime supplies into South Vietnam. It was referred to as a singular Ho Chi Minh trail; but it was really a spider web-like network of numerous trails. If one part of the trail were bombed, NVA trucks could be diverted to another part of the trail. The trails were concealed in densely vegetated rugged mountainous terrain. Bombing the Ho Chi Minh trail was sort of a cat and mouse contest between the Americans and the North Vietnamese. We were the cats on the prowl, and they were the mice scampering to hide from us. We joked that our bombings sometimes helped the NVA by clearing vegetation and busting up rocks from the sides of mountains so they could expand their road network. We amusingly speculated that the intense bombing campaign probably forced the NVA to use truck drivers that they let out of prison and chained into the trucks. It was hard to believe that anybody in their right mind would volunteer to drive a truck down those trails when an F-4 was flying overhead. Maybe they got a reprieve if they made it to South Vietnam.

My AC and I proceeded to our aircraft well ahead of the designated engine start time. I climbed the ladder to the cockpit, pulled the helmet out of my helmet bag, hooked up the oxygen hose and intercom cord, and set my helmet on the canopy railing. A quick preflight of the Martin Baker ejection seat confirmed that the safety pins were installed in both the ejection seat handles and the overhead curtain to prevent an inadvertent ejection while the aircraft was parked in the revetment.

Martin Baker ejection seats had generated a lot of respect because of their reliability in saving pilots. That seat had a phenomenal capability to extract pilots out of crippled aircraft both in the air and on the ground. If a burning aircraft were stationary on the ground, the ejection seat could catapult the pilot to an altitude high enough above the aircraft so that the parachute would open and safely float the pilot back to the ground. In the air, the ejection system was frequently used to extricate pilots from shot-up, unflyable aircraft.

I accomplished my walk around inspection of the ordnance. ACs checked the exterior of the aircraft while GIBs pre-flighted the bombs and missiles. The airplane crew chief followed us so he could immediately correct any problems. There rarely were any. There was no idle chatter between us; it was all business. Crew chiefs probably wondered why pilots did not talk to them, but a pilot's mind had to be focused on what was ahead. There was a certain degree of anxiety in all of this.

Bombs were loaded onto MERS (multiple ejection racks) attached to the underside of the wings. F-4 ordnance airmen were responsible for loading the bombs and they did an outstanding job of safely handling and installing those tremendously destructive man-made devices. Some ordnance guys had a sense of humor and wrote on the bombs with white chalk: *Merry Christmas Uncle Ho* or *here is a present for you.*

Ho, of course, referred to Ho Chi Minh, the communist leader of North Vietnam.

The front of each Mark 82 bomb had a small spinner that was shaped like a weathervane. In flight, the spinning vane enabled fuses within the bomb to be activated. On the ground, a safety pin was inserted into the vane, and it was removed prior to flight in the arming area at the end of the runway. One of my jobs when inspecting ordnance was to ensure the integrity of those vanes by removing the pin and spinning them. No pilot wanted to go through all the risks of flying a mission to Laos and end up dropping dud bombs. An additional safety for each bomb was electronically deactivated when the pilot flipped a switch in the cockpit that armed the weapons delivery system just prior to a drop.

There were several variations to the standard Mark 82 bomb. Some exploded on impact, such as the type of bombs loaded on our aircraft for this mission. One variant of this bomb had a delayed fuse installed so that it detonated at a preset amount of time after impact. Another was the Snake Eye bombs, with fins on the rear that extended to slow their rate of descent after they were released from the F-4. They were used on low-level bombing missions to allow an escape from the bomb blast so that the aircraft would not get blown out of the sky by the concussion force from its own bomb. There were also Mark 82s with three-foot-long fuse extenders on the front. They were nicknamed *daisy cutter bombs.* When the front of the long fuse contacted the ground, the bomb exploded about three feet above the ground. Rather than creating a deep crater, the explosion levelled an area, obliterating all living things within a 500-foot radius. They were frequently used to clear vegetation from an area to create helicopter landing zones. More than two million tons of Mk 82 bombs were dropped on Laos during the Vietnam War. With all that explosive firepower, it is a wonder that the country of Laos was not wiped off the face of the earth.

In addition to the bombs, each Gunfighter F-4 carried two Aim Seven radar-guided Sparrow air-to-air missiles, and two Aim Nine infrared guided Sidewinder air-to-air missiles. They were snugly fitted into the belly of the aircraft fuselage just under the F-4 engine intakes. The missiles were available to use in case we encountered Russian-made MIG aircraft.

I would be flying a newer F-4E model aircraft that was recently off the McDonnell Douglas production line in St. Louis, Missouri. The advantage of the E model versus earlier models was that it had an internal 20mm gun built into the nose of the aircraft. The older F-4D and C models had to carry the gun externally under the belly of the aircraft, which prohibited their ability to carry both a belly-mounted external fuel tank and a gun. Our E model external fuel tank was an oblong, bulbous-shaped 600-gallon fuel tank that provided fuel for about ten minutes of additional flight time. Our gun could be used against either an airborne Russian MIG aircraft, or it could be used against a target on the ground. It was hard to imagine being on the ground and having to experience the firepower of an F-4 Phantom blazing gun.

The F-4 was a mean looking machine that looked even meaner with shark's teeth painted on the nose. With eighteen 500-pound bombs slung under its wings, plus the gun and missiles, it had all the characteristics of an intimidating fighter/bomber aircraft.

In Vietnam, the F-4 was used in a variety of roles, but its primary role was bombing. If it were challenged by enemy aircraft, all the bombs and the fuel tank could be jettisoned so that the F-4 then became the most domineering fighter interceptor aircraft in the Vietnam theatre of air operations. Any time a Russian-made North Vietnamese MIG wanted to *play*, an F-4 pilot was more than ready to engage it in an air-to-air battle. F-4 pilots believed they were flying a machine with more power and more maneuverability than anything out there and had complete confidence in their airplane as well as their ability to fly it to its maximum capability. They did not strap *into* the airplane, they strapped the airplane *to their butt*.

MIG pilots were not anything to be underestimated. The MIG 17s and MIG 21s were close matches to the F-4 and some North Vietnamese pilots shot down enough US aircraft to qualify as aces with five kills. The MIG's limitation was that it had a short range, restricted high-altitude capability, and minimal loiter time, so they were not capable of executing long-lasting engagements. They were sort of like a dog trying to jump up and get a piece of meat out of your hand. They could make a couple of attempts to jump up and get you. If they were not successful, they gave up and went back to their base in Hanoi. The southern portion of Laos was out of their range. The NVA mostly kept their MIGs on the ground unless they detected American aircraft approaching Hanoi.

In 1969, the politicians in the United States decided that North Vietnam was off-limits for any bombing missions. F-4 pilots on bombing runs in Laos were prohibited from simply crossing the border into North Vietnam. The restriction necessitated more treacherous run-ins for us on Laotian targets. There were American radar operators monitoring our flight paths and they would turn us in to the higher-ups if we violated North Vietnamese airspace. This restriction, of course, was no secret to the North Vietnamese.

* * *

I plopped into my seat in our F-4 and snapped and jerked the ankle straps nice and tight. Shoulder straps were connected into a waist buckle and another strap was attached to the back of my helmet. The ankle and head straps were designed to pull a pilot's feet and head tight against the seat during an ejection. Flailing legs or a bobbling head could result in severe injuries during an ejection. My AC and I went through the preflight checks of our cockpit instruments in preparation for engine start. My AC gave the hand signal to the crew chief that he was ready to start the engines. Two fingers in a swirling motion was the signal for the crew chief to rev up the Huffer air-start unit that would send a surge of air into our engine to spin its jet turbines. At 10 percent rpm, my AC activated an ignition switch and moved the throttle forward to start the flow of fuel to the engine. The fuel burners in the engine combustion section ignited and there was the low roar of the right engine as it accelerated up to idle speed. Same procedure for the left engine.

I read the *before taxi* checklist challenge and response items. Then initiated contact with number two.

"Gunfighter Two-One flight check in."

"Twoop."

Distinctively pronouncing *two* did not have the right ring to it, so pilots added a *p* to the pronunciation of the number. If it were a four-ship formation, it would be said as "twoop," "threep," and four. It did not work to add *p* to four. Instead, four would sometimes get dragged out a few beats, sort of like there was disgust with being the last aircraft in the formation.

"Danang ground, Gunfighter Two-One, flight of two, taxi."

The crew chief was standing at attention in front of the aircraft with his arms crossed and ready to direct us out of the steel- and cement-reinforced, arch-style revetment. The AC flashed the taxi light, indicating that we were ready to taxi. The crew chief raised his arms and moved his hands back and forth, signaling that our aircraft was clear of obstructions and that the AC could begin to taxi. My AC slowly eased the throttles forward. Only the front seater had a nosewheel steering button. Depressing the button enabled the nose wheel to be steered using the rudder pedals. In an emergency, the back seater could steer the aircraft by applying differential wheel braking on the main gear like on a farm tractor, but it was rarely done to save on brake wear and tear.

Once clear of the revetment we pulled our ejection seat safety pins and displayed them to the crew chief. Each pin had a red flag attached to it so if he did not see the red flags, he would not salute but would cross his arms over his head and direct us to stop. This crew chief saw our flags, so he popped to attention and raised his right arm, giving us a professional military salute. He held his salute until my AC and I both returned it and he then waved us forward. We were off to the arming area at the end of the runway. Gunfighter 22, the number two aircraft in the formation, followed one aircraft length behind us.

The arming crew removed the munitions safety pins in the spinners and held them in the air for us to see. They made a quick check of the aircraft, bombs, and missiles, and gave a thumbs up that everything was okay.

We closed the canopies and completed the before-takeoff checklist.

"Gunfighter Two-One flight, go channel four"

"Twoop"

"Gunfighter Two-One flight, check in."

"Twoop"

F-4s used Ultra High Frequency (UHF) radios for communication. A pilot could manually tune in a frequency such as 275.8 for ground control or use a preset frequency that was coded to that specific UHF channel. The radios also had a pre-programmed frequency that all pilots in Southeast Asia continuously monitored. It was 243.0, which was the emergency frequency.

The time was 1000 hours.

I radioed Tower: "Gunfighter Two-One flight ready for takeoff."

The tower air traffic controller responded: "Gunfighter Two-One flight, taxi into position and hold."

The runway was 10,000 feet long. An F-4 fully loaded with bombs and fuel needed every bit of that runway to get airborne. While depressing the brake pedals, one throttle was slowly advanced to the stops to check engine instruments for signs of any problems. RPM–normal; EGT (exhaust gas temperature)–normal; fuel flow–normal; oil pressure–normal; exhaust nozzle position–one quarter; throttle retarded to idle; same for the other engine. Gunfighter 22 gave the thumbs up to signal that he was ready to go.

Tower gave us clearance. "Gunfighter Two-One flight, cleared for takeoff."

Both aircraft advanced the throttles to the first detent on the throttle quadrant while firmly standing on the brakes. Lead AC tapped his helmet as a preliminary signal to number two and positioned his head back against the headrest. He simultaneously thrust his head forward while releasing the brakes and advancing the throttles forward past the detent into the afterburner range. High volumes of fuel were pumped into an exhaust section of the engine, where it was ignited to provide a rapid increase in thrust. On lead's head throw forward, number two started the timer on his clock. Ten seconds later he released the brakes and started his takeoff roll. We were off to another combat mission, flying into Vietnam's jaws of war. Politicians back home tried to minimize the situation by calling it the Vietnam *conflict*. What a joke; this was a full-blown war.

POLITICAL BS

I was always patriotic and believed that it was personally rewarding to serve my country in Vietnam by fighting a war that I thought was just and right. It was, after all, a trying time in American history, when democracy was being tested against the threat of communism; and I believed in the preservation of our democracy. Democracy had given me the opportunity to go from a farm kid to a fighter pilot. I believed that under communism, this opportunity for self-advancement would never have existed. Communism represented the deficit of many freedoms that we Americans so dearly cherish.

Communist ideology entailed more than just the dictatorial elites imposing beliefs on their own people. These dictators wanted to control the world. The North Vietnamese leader, Ho Chi Minh, was a communist leader who was supported by Russia and China. Fear of the spread of communism led to development of President Eisenhower's domino theory, which became an early justification for US involvement in Vietnam. If Ho Chi Minh and his communist regime were successful in South Vietnam, what would prevent him and his Soviet counterparts from marching into other countries? John Foster Dulles, secretary of state for the Eisenhower administration stated: "If they [the Soviets] could get this peninsula of Indochina, Siam, Burma, Malaya, they would have what is called the rice bowl of Asia . . . And you can see that if the Soviet Union had control of the rice bowl of Asia that would be another weapon which would tend to expand their control into Japan and into India." Thailand was one country on the Indochina peninsula that was a firm ally of the United States. They granted permission for six US Air Force air bases at Ubon, Udorn, Nakhom Phanom (NKP), U-Tapao, Takhli and Korat. If Thailand fell to the communists, or even if it were bordered by communist countries, it would be a severe threat to democracy throughout the world.

South Vietnam was supposedly a democracy, but its leader, Nguyen Van Thieu, was belittled as being merely a puppet of the United States. Many South Vietnamese couldn't care less if they were governed by a democratic or a communist leader. The Viet Cong were South Vietnamese guerillas fighting in support of the communist North Vietnamese. Americans were not in Vietnam solely to fight a war for the freedom of the South Vietnamese people. We were there to fight a war to contain communism and preserve freedom in our own country. Our politicians seemed to be incapable of espousing this clear objective in Vietnam.

I was cynical about our politicians' motives for dragging out the war. Did they get us into the war to win? Or, were they trying to demonstrate their control over the military or maybe even subsidize a military hardware manufacturing industry? Was this just a big chess game for them, where they moved pawns around? Or were they truly sincere about the threat of communism and were just incompetent in developing a strategy to win? Military personnel were not allowed to publicly express their opinions, but there were strong private opinions among the F-4 pilots and considerable consternation about how the war was being conducted.

During one of Bob Hope's annual USO (United Service Organization) Christmas shows in Vietnam, his guest was Neil Armstrong, who had recently returned from his lunar landing. After his speech, a GI in the front row stood and asked him, "We all appreciate what you've done for our country, but can you tell us what we're doing here?"

Armstrong needed a long pause before he could come up with a response.

I developed some strong feelings toward politicians, especially when they tried to stick their noses into situations that they obviously were not qualified for, nor capable of directing. I, and many of my cohorts, viewed President Johnson and his cronies as incompetents who had no idea how to conduct a war. He proved it by dictating unreasonable restrictions on air operations over North Vietnam in 1967. Targets were selected by the president and secretary of defense over a White House lunch in Washington. They required F-105 and F-4 aircraft to fly a route along a ridge that ran parallel to the Red River on their run-in to targets around Hanoi. With this strategy, it did not take long for the NVA to figure out the American political stupidity, and to position their antiaircraft guns along that ridge. Flying into Hanoi for those American pilots was like running a gauntlet. That route became known as *thud ridge* because of the heavy losses of F-105 Thud aircraft. Many American pilots were sent to their deaths; or to years of prison and torture because of those idiotic types of decisions.

And what were the consequences of Johnson unilaterally imposing a bombing halt on North Vietnam on October 31, 1968? It enabled the NVA to stockpile military supplies in North Vietnam across the border from Laos and South Vietnam, knowing full well that the Americans were not going to do anything about it. Those were the supplies that were going to be used to kill Americans in South Vietnam, and some were probably the rockets that would be launched into Danang AB.

These were Johnson's words:

"By keeping a lid on all the designated targets, I knew I could keep the control of the war in my own hands. If China reacted to our slow escalation by threatening to retaliate, we'd have plenty of time to ease off the bombing. But this control—so essential for preventing World War III—would be lost the moment we unleashed a total assault on the North—for that would be rape rather than seduction—and then there would be no turning back. The Chinese reaction would be instant and total."

Johnson was trying to run a half-assed war with no clearly defined plan to win. The US had options that could have resulted in an early end to the war on favorable terms for our country. We could have mined the Haiphong Harbor, thereby cutting off supplies from Russia to the North Vietnamese. We could have bombed the Red River dikes and caused massive flooding of their rice paddies. Had we bombed the dikes in 1967 or 1968, most certainly civilian lives would have been lost; it was estimated that several thousand people would drown. While this sounds cruel, war in and of itself is cruel. In World War II, the Germans breached the dikes in Holland. In North Korea, the United States bombed the Toksan dam and destroyed the system that irrigated seventy five percent of their rice crop. We even dropped those nasty atomic bombs on Hiroshima and Nagasoki that caused an estimated 280,000 casualties, but it brought the Japanese to a surrender. By some estimates, dropping those atomic bombs preserved the lives of tens of thousands of Americans.

Because we were not decisive in our Vietnam War strategy, nearly 60,000 Americans lost their lives fighting a dragged-out war. Seventy percent of those American deaths occurred after Johnson's North Vietnam bombing halt in 1968. The lengthy war from 1965 to 1974 resulted in the death of more than two million North and South Vietnamese civilians with most of them likely occurring between 1968 and 1972. How could there be any reasonable justification for dragging out a war with continuing horrible consequences when our Air Force had the capability to end it quickly?

War is undeniably terrible. Every viable alternative should first be explored. If a country is going to fight a war, then fight it expeditiously, fight it ferociously, and fight it to win. Why jeopardize the lives of brave American soldiers and innocent civilians because you do not have the balls to do what needs to be done to get it over with? Our military was far superior to any in the world. As early as 1963, Admiral Henry D Felt, commander of American forces in the Pacific, stated in an article in *The New York Times* that Peking and Hanoi "don't want to fight the United States because they know how strong we are." Besides, the Chinese probably could not have cared less about Vietnam. Except for coal and rice, Vietnam had few natural resources of value to any country. Both the Chinese and Soviets were smart enough to never engage us in a world war over some third-world country. It was probably more advantageous for them to sit back and watch us wallow in our misery.

Dragging out that war for more than nine years led to diminishing public support back home for our war-fighting efforts. I was there for 365 days to do a job. Hopefully, I could then go home and forget about the asinine manner in which political cronies had directed the war. Unfortunately, going home was not always a pleasurable experience. Public frustration with the lengthy war was vented against returning military personnel.

In 1969, the ferocity and direction of the war effort changed when Nixon was elected president on a platform of ending the war in Vietnam. The war effort became more expansive and was not confined just to South Vietnam, as was thought back in the States. The secret bombing campaign over Laos increased in intensity, and the response from the NVA was equally intense. I was flying most of my missions into Laos, but the theatre of operations soon became even more expansive.

Later, in 1972, Nixon had the courage to intensely bomb targets in North Vietnam during Linebacker II. That eleven-day campaign resulted in an estimated loss of 1,600 North Vietnamese civilian lives, but it brought the North Vietnamese to the table to resume peace talks that resulted in the Paris Peace Treaty. Had we intensively bombed North Vietnam sooner and maybe even targeted the dikes or the harbor, one wonders how many more lives, both American and Vietnamese, could have been saved.

ADDITIONAL DUTY

Each mission involved planning, briefings, preflight, flying, and debriefing, which consumed about six to eight hours. There was still idle time, so we were expected to take on additional duties, such as conducting safety briefings, or working jobs in life support, awards and decorations, public affairs, or maintenance. We could even make up our own additional duty, such as escorting new guys around the base. I welcomed the opportunity to work in an additional duty because it helped to pass the time. It was a good distraction from the intensity of combat missions.

I was offered and accepted an additional duty to work in the frag shop located in the wing headquarters building. The frag order was a tasking that delineated each mission the 366 TFW would fly the next day. It was developed by headquarters 7th Air Force at Tan Son Nhut AB in Saigon. 7th AF was the primary command and control organization for the entire Air Force in Southeast Asia. The 366 TFW was under the command of 7th AF. The frag was a classified document that came in to the frag shop via a teletype machine in coded format. I had a top-secret security clearance, which granted me access to the codes so I could decode it and publish the need-to-know information in a readable format for each of the three flying squadrons. The squadrons posted their missions on a scheduling board and assigned the pilots to fly them. Maintenance personnel assigned airplanes to each mission and munitions loaded the airplanes with ordnance per my instructions. It was a well-coordinated effort on everyone's part.

The frag officer job was well suited for me: not much talking and a lot of thinking to prepare the plans for the entire next day Danang F-4 air war. The frag shop was manned twenty-four hours a day and each GIB worked twelve-hour shifts. I worked by myself and rotated shifts with six other GIBs. We communicated with each other via a logbook in which we documented significant events. We added a few personal comments: "Only 99 days to go. Double digit fidgets. Read it and weep." Signed: Joey

"YGBSM Joey. 311 days to go. OMG." Signed: George. YGBSM was shorthand for *you gotta be shittin' me*. I was envious of the double digiters. Someday, God willing, I would be in the double digits.

FREE TIME

Word spread fast that a C-130 cargo transport airplane was flying to Japan and that one of our squadron F-4 pilots was riding along. He took orders for stereo equipment, so I ordered a Teac reel-to-reel tape deck, record player, amplifier, reverberator, and some humongous speakers. When not working or flying, I copied and played audio recordings. I acquired music from the '50s, '60s, Christmas carols, and some very special songs and recordings about the Vietnam War. One was a recorded mission of F-4 pilots flying over North Vietnam who got mixed up with some North Vietnamese MIGs. The initial excitement in the AC's voice soon changed to a tone of utter terror when he realized that he was surrounded by a swarm of MIGs intent on his demise. He was never heard from again.

Some recordings used tongue-in-cheek humor to make a point. In one, a make-believe reporter interviewed a rather crusty fighter pilot. The reporter asked a series of questions, the pilot responded in a crass manner, and the reporter then tried to dignify those uncouth responses.

Reporter: "I suppose, Captain, that you've flown a certain number of missions over North Vietnam. What do you think of the SAMs used by the North Vietnamese?"

Captain: "Why, those bastards couldn't hit a bull in the ass with a bass fiddle. We fake the shit out of them. There's no sweat."

Reporter: "What the captain means is that the surface-to-air missiles around Hanoi pose a serious problem to our air operations and that the pilots have a healthy respect for them."

Reporter: "Tell me, Captain, have you flown any missions other than over North and South Vietnam?"

Captain: "You bet your sweet ass I've flown other missions. We get scheduled nearly every day on the trail in Laos where those bastards over there throw everything at you but the frickin' kitchen sink. Even the kids got slingshots."

Reporter: "What the captain means is that he has occasionally been scheduled to fly missions in the extreme western DMZ, and he has a healthy respect for the flak in that area."

Reporter: "What do you consider the most difficult target you've struck in North Vietnam?"

Captain: "The damn bridges. I must have dropped forty tons of bombs on those swayin' bamboo mothers, and I ain't hit one of them yet."

Reporter: "What the captain means is that interdicting bridges along enemy supply routes is very important and that bridges present quite a difficult target. The best way to accomplish this task is to crater the approaches to the bridge."

Reporter: "Thank you for your time, Captain."

Captain: "Screw you. Why don't you bastards print the real story, instead of all that crap?"

Reporter: "What the captain means is that he enjoyed this opportunity to discuss his tour with you."

I spent many hours in my room making recordings and listening to music. Even songs from the counterculture at Woodstock made their way to Danang, like the popular anti-Vietnam song by Country Joe and the Fish titled *I Feel Like I'm Fixin' to Die*.

BOMB DROP

We approached the Laotian border on our mission to Tchepone and completed the combat entry checklist, while taking special precaution to extinguish all exterior lights. We did not want to draw attention to ourselves with a flashing red beacon or a strobe that highlighted our aircraft. We headed to a tanker orbiting in an airborne racetrack pattern on the green track about 150 clicks (kilometers) west of the Ho Chi Minh trail. All Gunfighter F-4 missions to Laos were scheduled for air-to-air refueling from an Air Force KC135. The tanker was a military version of the four-engine Boeing 707. During air refueling training in California, we were taught to first establish radio contact with the tanker, then report that we were stabilized in position behind the tanker, then receive clearance to fly into air refueling position on the tanker. Those radio calls were never made in Vietnam. We just flew up to the tanker boom and started taking fuel.

The refueling boom consisted of a long telescoping tube that extended from under the rear belly of the tanker aircraft. It was attached to the tanker on an up/down and back/forth swivel mechanism. A smaller tube on the far end of the boom slid in and out of the larger tube. The forward/ aft extension of the smaller tube was marked on the boom with red, yellow, and green paint. It was the F-4 pilot's responsibility to keep his aircraft in the correct position directly behind the tanker. Optimum position was to keep the boom extension in the green. If the F-4 started to drop back, the boom would extend into the yellow; if it got into the red, the boom operator in the tanker would disconnect to prevent damage to his boom. Even in the worst of conditions with turbulence or heavy cloud cover, it was embarrassing for any pilot to get disconnected because he could not stay in position.

The refueling receptacle on the F-4 was on top of the fuselage, just behind the GIBs head. GIBs had an advantage over the AC in that they could see the boom extension directly above their head. The AC had to use the directional guidance lights under the belly of the tanker, so I flew most of the air-to-air refuelings.

There were a lot of *through the grapevine* stories in Vietnam and this one seemed credible: an F-111 had been shot up over hostile territory and could not maintain altitude on its own power due to battle damage. A tanker flew into the hostile area, connected with the F-111 and towed it out. I was skeptical about this story, so I decided to experiment with the tow capability of the tanker on one of my refueling hookups. Once connected to the boom, I very gradually eased off on the throttle until I felt a tug from the tanker. It did tow my aircraft. The tanker pilots did not like it because they had to counter my decreasing power by increasing the power on their aircraft, so I stopped doing it. At least I knew it was possible.

"Hillsboro, Gunfighter Two-One flight."

"Gunfighter Two-One flight, this is Hillsboro, go ahead."

"Gunfighter Two-One, flight of two, wall-to-wall Mark Eighty-twos, requesting clearance to target."

"Roger Gunfighter Two-One, you are cleared on target, go tactical, call off target with BDA."

Hillsboro was the callsign for an orbiting EC-130 ABCCC also referred to as AB triple C (airborne battlefield command and control center). At night, the callsign changed to *Moonbeam*. This EC-130 continuously orbited over western Laos, controlling missions into and out of target areas. BDA was the acronym for bomb damage assessment.

"Gunfighter Two-One flight, go tactical."

"Twoop."

Gunfighter 21 flight switched to the prearranged tactical radio frequency that was briefed in intel. There was no need to repeat it now just in case the enemy was monitoring our communications. This tactical frequency was a dedicated frequency for communications between Gunfighter 21 flight and the Covey 14 FAC who would be directing our airstrikes.

This FAC flew an O-2 aircraft or oscar deuce, as they were commonly called. It was a Cessna push-pull propeller-driven airplane. O-2 pilots searched the area for suspicious activity that would make good targets for F-4 strike missions. When they spotted something of significance, they directed F-4 pilots to strike the target.

The FACs flew low and slow over enemy territory. Since they were targeting enemy positions on the ground for destruction, they must have been a prime target for the NVA gunners. Yet, they were always there, doing their job with the highest degree of professionalism. Those O-2 FAC pilots were talked about as having a big pair of . . . well, you know what.

There was another group of FACs known as Stormy FACs that flew F-4s out of Danang. When they spotted enemy activity, they marked the target with a flare, and called in F-4s with bombs for an airstrike. Stormy FACs were fast, so they could cover a lot of area in a short period of time. Because of their speed, they also missed a lot of enemy ground activity. The F-4 was notorious for leaving a trail of smoke, so they were easily spotted by the enemy and it resulted in high losses of Stormy aircraft and pilots.

Stormy FACs were an elite group of pilots, so participation would have been good fodder for my evaluation report that would be written at the end of my tour. I thought about applying for it, but I decided to do some research first. One Stormy GIB was a close friend and we discussed a couple of incidents he had experienced. On one, his AC took a direct hit to the cockpit, so he had to land the blood-spattered F-4 from the back seat. On another mission he had a hole shot through his checklist that was laying on the dash in front of him. It seemed like Stormy FACs had a bullseye on them, so I decided not to pursue it.

"Covey One-four, Gunfighter Two-One flight."

"Roger, Gunfighter Two-One flight, Covey One Four, go ahead."

"Gunfighter Two-One, flight of two with wall-to-wall Mark Eighty-twos."

"Roger, Gunfighter, report in sight."

There was no need to tell the FAC we were F-4s since Gunfighters were well-known throughout Southeast Asia as the F-4s out of Danang.

"Covey, give me a hold down."

I was instructing the Covey FAC to hold down his transmit button so that his aircraft sent a directional signal to the ADF (automatic direction finder) navigation radio in my aircraft. A needle on my ADF instrument pointed to Covey's location.

"In sight, ten o'clock low." I specified ten o'clock so that our wingman knew where to look for him. Both aircrew needed to acquire a visual on the FAC.

"Roger Gunfighter, stand by for target briefing."

Expediency was important because fully loaded F-4s burned a lot of fuel. With a full load of ordnance, an F-4 burned 6000 pounds or close to 900 gallons of fuel per hour. If we had to use afterburners to evade enemy gunfire, the fuel burn could easily increase to ten times that rate and deplete our fuel in a short period of time. For that reason, we only used afterburners when we needed immediate acceleration.

"Ready to copy target briefing."

"Gunfighter Two-One flight, your target is a truck convoy exiting a mountain pass from North Vietnam. The trucks are in the open now but will soon be entering an area of heavy ground cover, so we need to hit them as soon as possible. Target elevation is seven eight zero feet. Altimeter setting two-niner decimal eight-seven. Suggested run-in is from south to north. Numerous triple A sites are concentrated to the east of the target. If you take a hit, recommended egress is to the northwest. I am putting down a smoke. Advise when you have it in sight."

We were flying a circular orbit over the FAC at 15,000 feet. The Covey FAC shot a white smoke flare from his aircraft that he deliberately aimed some distance from the target. It was intentional so that the smoke would not alert the enemy truck drivers that they were being targeted.

"Roger, Covey, smoke in sight."

"The convoy is two hundred meters to the east of my smoke. When you are ready, you are cleared in."

Targets frequently changed from the preplanned target, depending on observations of the FAC. We recomputed our pickle altitude to base it on the elevation of the new target. My AC turned a switch that selected the six bombs we would be dropping for the first pass; three each from a MER under each wing. He flipped another switch to remove the safeties so that the bombs were armed.

"Lead's in."

My AC rolled our F-4 up on its wingtip and we began a sixty-degree dive toward the ground. He rapidly changed the aircraft flight path (jinked) while I called out altitudes and airspeeds. My head was on a swivel, looking for enemy gunfire and SAM launches. Airspeed was rapidly increasing toward the upper bomb drop limit of 500 knots. We did not want to go supersonic or it would throw the bombs off their trajectory. Approaching the release altitude, I called out: "Ready, ready, *pickle.*"

There was a thump as the bombs released. The aircraft pitched up from the sudden release of 3,000 pounds of weight. My hand was behind the stick. If it did not come back immediately after the release, I was ready to take control of the aircraft. In such a steep descent, the aircraft continues to lose considerable altitude until its downward trajectory is reversed. There could be no delay; pull up immediately or end up splattering yourself across the ground.

A pilot could become so intent on putting the bombs on target that he disregarded the need to pull up in a timely manner. It was called target fixation and my job was to prevent that from happening. Most ACs respected their GIBs if they took control of the aircraft when they pressed below pickle altitude. There was one AC who thought that GIBs should not touch the stick. I made up my mind that I did not care what that guy thought; I was going to do whatever I needed to do to save my butt. If there were any questions, my squadron commander would back me up. My hand was always behind the stick, ready to take over in a split second.

It was possible that instead of being fixated on the target, the AC could be incapacitated. If I did not take immediate action, both of us would be dead.

Immediately after the bomb release, my AC sucked the stick back into my groin. The forces inflated my G suit, but I still momentarily blacked out because we exceeded its capability. The 6 Gs put a severe strain on my neck. Rapid horizontal and vertical jinking forces flung me up, down, and laterally against my shoulder harness.

The AC continued jinking until we reached a safe altitude. I looked back and could see the bombs exploding on the ground. After three passes we were out of bombs, and we were bingo fuel, so it was time to head back to Danang.

Covey flew over the target and did a damage assessment.

"Gunfighter Two-One flight, are you ready for your BDA report?"

"Roger Covey, ready to copy."

"Gunfighter Two-One, all bombs on target, five trucks destroyed, numerous trucks disabled, some secondary explosions, nice job, have a good day."

I would relay this information to Airborne Battlefield Command and Control Center (ABCCC) after exiting the target area. The BDA was one bit of intelligence gathered by 7th AF that was useful for developing a subsequent frag. If we had not destroyed those trucks, they could retarget that area.

I took over the controls and flew the aircraft back to Danang. Approaching the base, Danang approach control established radar contact with our flight, and assigned individual radar vectors to Gunfighter 21 and 22 to separate us into single ship flights for the approach and landing to runway 17. We were not permitted to land as a formation. The approach controller transmitted headings that would align our aircraft with the runway. Ten miles from the end of the runway, the approach controller turned us over to a final GCA (ground-controlled approach) controller who provided us with vertical as well as horizontal guidance.

The approach to Runway 17 took our flight between two mountainous peaks located ten miles off the end of the runway. The peak on the eastern side was called Monkey Mountain. The US military controlled that peak and installed a huge bulbous radar site on top of it. The peak to the west was at the end of a ridgeline that was rumored to be infested with VC, who took occasional pot shots at vulnerable low, slow-flying aircraft on final approach to Danang. It was defoliated with Agent Orange and heavily patrolled by gunship aircraft. Civilian airliners shuttling troops in and out of Vietnam flew that same approach to Danang.

"Gunfighter Two-One, this is your final controller. How copy?"

"Roger, have you loud and clear."

"Gunfighter Two-One, no need to acknowledge further transmissions. If no transmission is received for five seconds, take over visually or execute a missed approach. Missed approach heading is one-eight-zero degrees. Climb to and maintain two thousand feet. Contact approach control on two-eight-eight decimal eight. Turn left to one-six-eight degrees. Begin descent in one mile."

"Turn left to one-six-six degrees; begin descent."

"Right to one-six-eight degrees; drifting slightly below glide slope."

"Right to one-seven-one degrees; approaching glide slope."

"On course, on glide slope."

"On course, on glide slope."

"On course, drifting slightly below glideslope."

The instructions continued until we reported either the runway in sight or we descended to a decision height altitude.

"Approaching decision height. Report runway in sight or execute a missed approach."

On short final, my AC reported: "Runway in sight."

Normally, ACs would take control of the aircraft and land. A few ACs were sort of laid back and would tell me to just go ahead and land.

The runway had a steep crown. If there was moisture on the runway, it was very slick and we could slide off the side of it. On rainy days, we lowered our tail hook to capture a cable arresting system that was stretched across the end of the runway. A two-inch thick wire cable was raised a couple of inches above the runway by rubber donuts so that our hook could get under it and snag it. It was important to lock our shoulder harness prior to landing because our rate of deceleration went from 150 knots to zero in about two seconds. Instead of bringing the throttles to idle after landing, we went to full thrust in case we missed the cable. We could then go around and make another attempt to land. After we were stopped on the runway, airmen were positioned on both ends of the cable and they activated a hydraulic winch to tow us backwards to remove tension from the cable. On their command, we raised the tail-hook, and taxied clear of the runway. The entire procedure was expertly completed in a matter of seconds.

Back on the ramp, we shut down the engines, unstrapped, climbed down the ladder, and inspected our F-4 for battle damage. I was mentally and physically exhausted.

BOXER 22 SAR

On December 5, 1969, I was working the afternoon shift in the frag shop. The previous frag officer had already done most of the work of decoding the frag and assigning missions to the squadrons. Major changes started coming in, such as redoing the entire ordnance loads on nearly all the aircraft. What was going on that dictated such dramatic changes?

Two Air Force F-4 pilots were in an extremely critical situation after being shot down over Laos. They were down in a heavily infested enemy troop area. Both downed pilots were in contact with the search and rescue (SAR) commander via their handheld VHF radios. Normal bombing of the Ho Chi Minh trails was halted as the Air Force dedicated any necessary resources to get those pilots out. I was scheduled to fly the next day and would be a part of that SAR effort.

The SAR commander's tactical callsign was *Sandy One.* He was flying an A1E aircraft, which was a fierce-looking, single seat propeller attack aircraft, much like the fighter-type aircraft used in WWII. He functioned as an intermediary between the downed pilots and the strike aircraft. Inputs from the pilots were used to identify enemy personnel for targeting. For this SAR, there were plenty of targets to take out before those pilots could be rescued. The pilots were shot down late in the day, so the SAR was terminated the first day because of darkness. The SAR commander instructed the downed pilots to find a good place to hide for the evening, turn off their radios to conserve battery power, and to reestablish contact the next morning.

By daybreak the next day, I was flying in one of several orbiting four-ship F-4 flights loaded with ordnance. We were stacked in holding patterns every 1,000 feet awaiting our turn to be called in on a target by Sandy. The Air Force was committed to getting those pilots out. The bad guys seemed to be equally dedicated to get to those pilots. Some bad guys were so close to them that Sandy could not call in air strikes on them for fear the bombs would kill the pilots. A few clicks from all this activity, a Jolly Green Giant rescue helicopter was orbiting and ready to swoop in at a moment's notice to pluck the downed pilots out of the jungle.

The rescue attempt was unsuccessful the first day. For the downed AC, it turned into a tragedy when the bad guys got to him. The GIB heard his screams, and then his radio went dead. With no radio contact, and no beeper, flare or other evidence of him being alive, the SAR effort for him came to a halt.

The GIB was instructed to turn off his radio and find a good hiding place for a second night. The next day at daybreak, the rescue effort continued. Later in the day after several bombing strikes, the Sandy pilot decided that the area had been cleared enough of bad guys so that the Jolly Green could get in to retrieve him. The helicopter hovered over a clearing and the GIB ran toward the helicopter. Ground fire from the enemy suddenly got intense. It was so intense that the helicopter needed to get out of there or risk getting shot down. For the downed pilot, it meant another night of hiding in the jungle.

The third day, contact was reestablished with the downed pilot and, after clearing a helicopter landing area, another attempt was made to get the Jolly Green helicopter in for a rescue. They were able to hover long enough to lower a PJ (para jumper) on a sling. The PJ hooked up the downed GIB, gave a thumbs up signal, and Boxer 22 and the PJ were safely sucked out of that enemy infested jungle.

The GIB later reported that during the second night, the bad guys had gotten so close to him that they almost stepped on his hand. The dense jungle foliage and his gray flight suit helped to conceal his location. There was a great deal of love and respect for those Jolly Green Giant helicopter crewmembers who put their butts on the line to pluck F-4 pilots out of enemy infested areas. A Jolly Green crewmember never had to pay for a drink at a bar when F-4 pilots were around.

TAKE NO PRISONERS

The frag job was a good distraction from the war but there was still free time. I meditated while listening to music or got together with other GIBs in one of our rooms to reminisce or maybe start some rumors. I had developed close friendships with several of them. If one heard something of interest, it was shared by all. During one of these get-togethers, one hot topic was the missions to Laos and the perception that F-4 pilots were getting their *butts shot off*. It was rumored, and somewhat confirmed by a downed GIB who was rescued, that the NVA were not taking prisoners. The dense jungle trails evidently did not make it worth the effort for the bad guys to transport a pilot POW from Laos back to Hanoi. The North Vietnamese already had more than an adequate supply of POWs from the 1968 Operation Rolling Thunder bombing campaign over North Vietnam.

Rumor was that the NVA were torturing captured pilots before killing them. They grabbed the pilot's hand-held VHF radio and held the transmit button down to broadcast his screams as they tortured him. It was probably good that F-4 pilots could not monitor the hand-held VHF radio frequency. The Sandy's could monitor it, and if true, it must have been terrifying for them. The methods of torture seemed unnecessarily cruel. It was obviously intended to break the spirit of American pilots. The gruesome rumor was that one pilot had been skinned and on another they cut off . . . well, we will leave it at that. Just the thought of it brought back memories of the state fair incident when I was younger, and it made me tremble. So much for being a macho fighter pilot. How could humans be so cruel toward one another? Then again, how could anyone drop those nasty Mark 82 bombs and napalm on other human beings, killing and maiming them? Damn the political leaders who cannot get their act together so we can all live in peace.

Combatants in war were supposed to abide by rules of the Geneva Convention Article 42:

1. "No person parachuting from an aircraft in distress shall be made the object of attack during his descent.

2. Upon reaching the ground in territory controlled by an adverse Party, a person who has parachuted from an aircraft in distress shall be given an opportunity to surrender before being made the object of attack, unless it is apparent that he is engaging in a hostile act."

The Vietnamese enemy probably never heard of the Geneva Convention rules and even if they did, they could care less. After our discussion was over, I meditated over the need to develop a plan in case I was shot down and facing capture. I formulated my options. First, I could hope that the rumors were not true and that the bad guys would capture me and send me to Hanoi. This was unlikely since only about 2 percent of the pilots shot down in Laos were taken as POWs to Hanoi. Besides, the treatment of POWs by the North Vietnamese was brutal, with frequent torture to the point of near death. Perhaps a quicker death in Laos might be a better option.

Second, I could shoot it out with the bad guys. Then again, my .38 revolver only held six rounds of ammunition, and there were armies of North Vietnamese troops in Laos with Russian made AK-47 rifles and lots of ammunition. Even if I took some of them out, it might tick off the rest of them, and they could make dying even worse for me. So, that was not a good plan.

Third, I could turn the .38 on myself. This was a possibility, but not a good option because it conflicted with my religious beliefs. Man did not have a right to take his own life; death was in the hands of God, so committing suicide was a one-way ticket to hell.

Finally, I could maybe endure the torture to the point of passing out. After all, how long does it take for a man to die? Most likely this was my only option. Dang, this was a nasty war.

I worried about getting out of Vietnam alive, so I turned to my trusted accomplice, the Lord. I prayed at night before going to sleep. Then I sort of forgot about him during the day because it seemed like I was too busy with other matters. Obviously, I was not a very faithful follower. Hopefully, he would understand.

OH NO

The mission for my squadron changed from daytime FAC controlled missions to nighttime self-FAC missions. Our callsign changed from *Gunfighter* to *Night Owl*. Each mission was single ship and was assigned a specific area to patrol. In addition to armament, our F-4s were loaded with high-candlepower flares that could be used to illuminate suspected enemy locations.

I was paired with a first lieutenant AC who earned his front seat assignment when he graduated first in his pilot training class. He was a top-notch pilot who was humble and showed considerable respect toward me. By now, I had enough missions under my belt that I was considered an old head, and it felt good to be respected for my experience, abilities, and personality.

Prior to entering Laos, in addition to extinguishing our wingtip navigation lights, strobes, and rotating beacons, we also dimmed our cockpit lights so as not to illuminate ourselves to the enemy. The F-4 was notorious for its smoke trail, which was like a pointer in the sky for the enemy to locate us. One advantage of night flying was that this smoke trail was not visible to the enemy gunners.

We were assigned to work an area on the trail called Delta 45. There was a dense network of trails in that area. Initially, we focused on detecting lights on the ground, or spotting a moving silhouette. If we suspected activity, we rolled in and dropped a flare to illuminate the area and try to get a visual on the target.

Our munitions consisted of Mk 82 bombs and CBUs (cluster bomb units). The CBU was a canister bomb with a timed fuse. It was released at a precise altitude so that it opened a short distance above the ground. When the cannister blew open, it released several little bomblets about the size of hand grenades. Some of those bomblets exploded immediately on the ground; others exploded over time. If we were getting intensely fired upon (*hosed down*, in fighter pilot lingo), and if we could spot the approximate location of the enemy antiaircraft artillery (AAA), we would roll in with the CBUs to quiet things down before bombing a target.

Night flying enabled me to learn the different types of AAA because both the tracers and the red fiery shells were visible. Every tenth shell fired from an enemy AAA gun was a tracer shell. Tracers had a pyrotechnic charge that burned bright. Tracers enabled the gunners to see where their bullets were going in the air; likewise, pilots could see those tracers heading toward them and could take evasive action.

A 23mm gun had a quick burst of firing that could reach an altitude of 10,000 feet. The 37mm and 57mm guns had a slower rate of fire and higher altitude capability before their tracers started dipping downward. It was not uncommon to see a mix of all three types of guns shooting at the same time. Occasionally a slower-firing 85mm or 100mm radar-guided gun could be spotted, but they were usually positioned closer to the North Vietnam border since they were not as mobile as the smaller guns. When big guns did show up in Laos, they would usually be positioned in a concealed area, such as a cave with a rail system so that the enemy could roll the gun in and out of the cave. The guns had a high-altitude capability extending upward from 25,000 feet to 35,000 feet. Since the F-4 could not readily climb to those altitudes to escape, we had to try to break the tracking solutions of those gunners by performing high G horizontal and vertical maneuvers.

Night missions enabled us to view the expansive aerial display of antiaircraft gunfire across eastern Laos. It seemed to light the sky like

Fourth of July fireworks. The ZPU 23 gunners were a significant threat because there were lots of them, and they could fire one hundred or more rounds before they had to stop to let their gun barrels cool. The gunners on the 37mm and 57mm guns seemed to shoot aimlessly at any noise in the air. The 85 mm guns were controlled by radar, so those gunners did not need visual contact with our aircraft. Even without a radar lock on, they seemed to be intent on shooting us down. We used to joke that gunners were probably rewarded with a free vacation to a beach resort on the Gulf of Tonkin if they shot down an F-4.

Even though we derogatorily referred to the enemy as gooks, gomers, charlie, or slant eyes, there was respect for their capability to conduct low-technology warfare against a formidable foe. Our Night Owl missions initially produced a lot of secondary explosions when we dropped bombs on lights on the ground. After a few weeks of night missions, there were fewer lights and fewer secondary explosions. An F-4 was a noisy airplane, so it appeared that they turned off their lights when they heard us and ran their trucks down the Ho Chi Minh trail blacked out. They then tried to entice us into bombing well-lit dummy targets that they had surrounded with their antiaircraft guns.

One night, we were pulling off from a heavily contested target when our aircraft suddenly lurched into an uncontrollable attitude.

I was alarmed and directed some rapid-fire comments to the AC: "What's going on? Are we hit? Check engine instruments. Let's get the hell out of here."

My AC struggled to regain control of the aircraft. He lit the afterburners, which rocketed our F-4 in whatever direction the aircraft wanted to go. The afterburner used lots of JP-4 fuel that was dumped into the fuel injectors on the engine. When the fuel was ignited it created a rocket-like acceleration. It lit up the sky with a long stream of fire streaking from the rear of our aircraft. The afterburners burned a lot of precious fuel that was needed to get us to a safe destination.

After some struggles and attempts at finding the right stick position in both the front and rear cockpit, we got the aircraft to become awkwardly controllable but responses to control inputs were far from normal. I switched over to Guard frequency 243.0, which entailed just a quick flick of the switch.

"Mayday, Mayday, Mayday. Night Owl Two-One declaring emergency."

Moonbeam, the ABCCC that controlled night missions over Laos, responded immediately: "Night Owl Two-One, this is Moonbeam. What's the nature of your emergency?"

His radio transmission had an amazingly calm inflection. Mine, however, expressed a certain degree of anxiety as I described the control issues we were experiencing with our F-4. In the background, I could overhear another Moonbeam controller directing other F-4s toward our position in case we had to punch out. SAR aircrews were alerted for a possible recovery mission. The Air Force spared no effort to ensure the preservation of their aircrews. It was a great relief when we got our squirrely F-4 over the Plaine Des Jarres of Laos, which was a relatively safe area as we headed toward Ubon AB, Thailand. Engine instruments appeared normal and it seemed like it was some type of hydraulic failure that was affecting our flight controls. We had burned through a lot of fuel when we lit the afterburners. To make it to Ubon, we needed to *hit* a tanker.

My AC found a stick position that resulted in reasonable control of the aircraft, but it was considerably different than the normally centered position. We were able to hook up to the tanker, get the much-needed fuel, and arrive at Ubon for an uneventful landing. A positive outcome was that we got to spend a couple of nights in Thailand.

Ubon was the favorite divert location for Danang pilots. Pilots experiencing the slightest mechanical malfunction used it as an excuse to divert to Ubon. It worked until higher-ups decided to publish guidelines on what constituted a legitimate reason to divert to Ubon. Obviously, a shot up aircraft was still a valid reason.

The enormity of decision-making placed on young men flying the F-4 was unfathomable. Most of us were in our 20s, some were in their 30s, and a few in leadership positions were in their 40s. I was astounded that the Air Force trusted me, this twenty-seven-year-old former farm kid, with the responsibility to fly a new multimillion-dollar, high-tech aircraft for my country. I was proud and honored to participate in this critical effort to stop the spread of communism.

ANOTHER PILOT DOWN

F-4 losses were significant. Estimates were between 445 and 528 F-4s were lost during the Vietnam War. One of my pilot training classmates was shot down near the North Vietnam border. I learned about it during one of my mission intel briefings.

"A review of yesterday's Southeast Asia hot sheet shows that an F-4 was lost out of Ubon. It was lost over the Ban Karai Pass in Laos. His wingman noted that they had spotted some trucks on the ground. Approximately thirty seconds later, a large fireball was observed on the ground. There were no chutes and no radio contact, so they are listed as MIA (missing in action)."

One of those pilots was Bob Gomez who was a classmate who sat at my table in pilot training and a close friend. [His status has since been changed to KIA (killed in action). May God be with you, my friend].

* * *

I was scheduled to fly a SAR support mission in the northern part of Laos. Once again, the air war over Laos had come to a near standstill to get one of the pilots out of a heavily infested enemy area. There was no contact with the other pilot. He was either killed by the enemy or died from injuries caused by the ejection. In an ejection, many bad things could happen. Parachuting down into the tall trees in the jungle was hazardous. The chute could hang up in the trees, leaving the pilot dangling several feet above the ground and making him a sitting duck for enemy marksmen. Descending through the heavy jungle vegetation could also tear up a pilot's body. Landing on rugged terrain often resulted in broken bones. The ejection itself had a high degree of risk, with some pilots experiencing a broken back or severe injuries to their necks when the explosive force propelled their body upward and out of the aircraft.

Any time a pilot was shot down, the Air Force made every effort to locate the pilot either via his radio or his radio beacon, which sent out a locator signal. SAR personnel looked for evidence of life, such as flares, a fire, signaling mirror flashes, patterns of twigs or rocks, visual contact, or whatever else was available for the downed pilot. Minus these signs, the SAR commander still scoured the area for any sign of life from the pilot until he was convinced that there was no hope. Without any evidence of life, there was no SAR effort. Possibly, some pilots were left behind in the Laotian jungle with no hope for rescue due to incapacitation or inability to summon for help.

This SAR effort focused solely on the one pilot who was in communication with Sandy. Sandy had spotted enemy troops moving in his direction and the downed pilot could hear them coming. They were getting very close. Our flight of two F-4s was orbiting overhead so Sandy called us in on a target. He marked the target with a smoke that he shot directly into the enemy troops hoping that it would deter their advance.

I was flying with a new AC. He selected a bomb delivery method that had rarely been used in Laos on any mission, much less a SAR effort. It was called dive toss. It permitted us to do a stand-off release of the bombs without having to fly directly over the target at a low altitude. Dive toss lessened our exposure to AAA in the target area. As we were setting up for our run-in, I selected a mode on my radar that displayed a pencil-width ground return. The AC rolled in on the target and aligned the pipper with the smoke on the ground while I locked onto the ground return. When his sight was stabilized on the target, the AC pickled the bombs, but the bombs did not immediately release, which was by design. We began our escape maneuver while our onboard computer continuously updated the programmed bomb release. When the computer determined that the correct bomb release parameters had been met, it released the bombs. By then we were already climbing to a safe altitude. While this sounded good in theory, it was not always the best option in the real world. Dive toss was probably more appropriate for delivering nuclear weapons because it enabled the aircrew to start their escape maneuver far in advance of the bomb exploding so that the aircraft would not get blown out of the sky by its own bomb. Our F-4 weapons release computer system (WRCS) was developed with 1950s technology and, for Vietnam operations, there were some limitations.

I felt the bombs release during our pull up. It was followed soon thereafter by an angry radio transmission from Sandy.

"Gunfighter Two-One, what the fuck are you doing? Your bombs were way long. You probably just killed him."

Pilots never used foul language over the radio, but this was a situation whereby the SAR commander evidently believed it was necessary. We did not respond and there seemed to be an eternal silence. Radio frequencies during a SAR were not to be cluttered with excuses. F-4 pilots were simply expected to put their bombs on target. I knew that the dive toss mode had rarely been used in Laos, so experimenting with its use on a SAR effort was not a good decision. I should have recognized this and informed the new AC, but I did not.

Our F-4 had been airborne for over an hour so the spinning gyro and pendulum mechanism that fed inputs to the weapons release system evidently drifted out of alignment and accumulated an error caused by our aircraft maneuvering. There was no cockpit indicator for us to determine its accuracy. It appeared that our computer had developed a substantial error and it released the bombs late, so they were tossed long in the direction of the downed pilot.

"Gunfighter Two-One, stand by while I go off frequency and see if I can contact the downed pilot."

I was feeling very, very sick to my stomach. I had never puked in an airplane, but I was ready to do so now. Did I just kill a fellow American, an F-4 pilot just like me? I had this helpless feeling of not being able to do anything to rectify the situation, so I could only hope and pray. Yes, I did say a prayer during a wartime mission that the very worst did not happen.

Sandy came back on frequency and chills went through my spine when he started his transmission:

"Gunfighter Two-One."

There was an extraordinarily long pause like he was trying to put his thoughts together. SAR commanders seemed to develop a close emotional attachment to downed pilots. Often, they tried to draw enemy fire toward themselves to distract the enemy from pursuing the pilot. It made the enemy reveal their location so Sandy could direct strikes against them. The bravery of Sandy pilots was hard to comprehend.

"I just established radio contact with the pilot on the ground and he said 'Thanks.' The bombs were so close that they sent the bad guys scrambling."

I could not keep the tears of relief from flowing. Thank God no one saw me. Our bomb drop worked out for the good of the downed pilot, but it was a little too close for the SAR commander. He no longer had confidence in us to put our bombs on target.

"Gunfighter Two-One, you need to go home. You are no longer wanted here."

We returned to Danang with bombs still hanging. Word about the incident got back to Danang faster than our aircraft and we were met at the aircraft by the wing commander, a full colonel. He hollered up at us while we were still in the aircraft.

"I want to see both of you in my office, ASAP."

My hands were shaking as I struggled to unfasten my shoulder straps and leg restraints. I was anticipating the worst as I shuffled my wobbly legs into the wing commander's office and popped a somewhat unprofessional salute to the colonel.

"So, boys, tell me what happened."

The conversation started out reasonably civil. It was not the screaming or butt-chewing I was expecting. The wing commander listened intently as

I attempted to get words out of my mouth that made sense. Even though I was a GIB, I was equally responsible, or possibly more so, because I was an old head GIB. I was expecting the wing commander to ground me. Evidently, I came up with the right words and convinced him that this incident was not totally our fault since there were no restrictions on the use of dive toss in Southeast Asia. The wing commander decided that it was a *learn from* mistake that could not happen again. The next day, signs were posted in the briefing area.

DIVE TOSS PROHIBITED ON SAR MISSIONS.

Both of us were cleared to resume flying duties, and the downed pilot was successfully rescued, possibly with the help of our misplaced bombs. I am sure that the rescued pilot and I both agree that there has to be a God.

ROCKETS INCOMING

There were hundreds, perhaps even thousands of US personnel stationed at Danang AB who were subjected to frequent rocket attacks. Danang AB was nicknamed *Rocket City*. One night, while working in the frag shop, I overheard radio transmissions in the command post that Cam Rahn AB, Vietnam was under attack. Within a few minutes, I heard the whistling sound of airborne rockets followed by a loud thud. The attacks always occurred at night, probably because it provided cover of darkness for the VC who ignited the fuses on the rockets. A report came in from one 366 TFW unit that there was damage to the enlisted personnel barracks. Another report came in that a rocket landed on top of an F-4 revetment just a short distance from the wing headquarters building. That rocket bounced off the top of the revetment and left a big pock mark in the cement encasing it. There was debris scattered all over the ramp area but no damage to the F-4. A crew chief working inside that revetment said the noise was deafening. In addition to the material damage, the rocket attacks inflicted damage of another kind. They created fear in everyone that their lives could be snuffed out at any moment.

Recovery folks did not cordon off disaster areas or try to hide anything, so the next day I walked over to see the damage to the enlisted barracks. One end of the barracks was demolished. I never heard how many were killed but anyone who was in that end of the barracks at the time most certainly went home to their loved ones in a box.

* * *

The men's toilet in the squadron building had three urinals. The center urinal was always clean, sort of like it was not being used. I used only the left or right urinal and I thought that it was only me. Then I noticed that other guys would also wait in line for the left or right urinal even though the center urinal was available. Urinal preference became the subject of one of our GIB meetings. It turned out, it was either the left or right urinal for everybody and never the center urinal. F-4 pilots were superstitious.

ENTERTAINING
THE TROOPS

There was frequent entertainment at the O Club (Officers Club). Some USO (United Service Organization) performers were good; some not so good. There was a lot of hooting and hollering during the show but absolutely no booing even when the performers were bad. Pilots had a lot of respect for those performers who were willing to come to Danang and risk their lives to put on a show for us. We all joined in when they sang the chorus to *Detroit City* (*I Want to Go Home*) written by Danny Dill and Mel Tillis. Toward the end of the show, after lots of beer, it did not matter if the performers were good or bad; all of us were singing at the top of our lungs to a song by Eric Burdon and The Animals titled *We Gotta Get Out of This Place*.

Food at the O Club kind of sucked. A bunch of us guys would sometimes head over to the Marine side of the base where there was a buffet line with salad, potatoes, bread, and grilled steaks. Although the steaks were good, they were not as good as Ma's pan-fried steaks from the steer that Dad butchered on the farm.

Another favorite restaurant was located off base at China Beach. The beach had beautiful white sand and the food in the restaurant was okay. It was a rest and relaxation (R&R) location for US personnel in Vietnam although it was hard to imagine why anyone would want to stay in Vietnam on their R&R. It was just a few clicks from Danang at the end of a road that meandered through an area of densely populated Vietnamese shacks. Some Vietnamese kids had obviously been taught to hate Americans, so they threw rocks at our bread truck. One banged so loud that it sounded like a hand grenade explosion, or maybe that is what it was. Kids tried to reach in through the side window to grab the the driver's watch. After the novelty of going to the beach wore off, I decided it was best to just stay put at Danang.

Military grooming standards were oftentimes ignored in Vietnam. Back in the States, mustaches were permitted but they needed to be trimmed so they did not extend beyond the upper lip. In Vietnam, some pilots let it grow out to form handlebars. No commander in his right mind would discipline an F-4 pilot for violating grooming standards for mustaches. Beards, however, were not permitted because facial hair interfered with the seal of the oxygen mask against a pilot's face.

* * *

Shortly after I got to Danang, I was told it would be stylish to wear a custom-made party suit to the squadron parties. All the old heads had one. The party suit was an Air Force blue colored flight suit with name, rank, and the 366 TFW gunfighter patch embroidered on it. The patch depicted the official F-4 mascot, *the spook*. He was a short character with big feet and large eyes staring out from under the brim of a tall black witch's hat. Slung under his arm was a blazing gun pod that was bigger than he was.

Every month the squadron held a party at the O club to say goodbye to departing pilots. Everybody who had one wore their party suits. We knew that there would be no party or parades for us when we got back home to the States. When a pilot returned from his last mission, he was hosed down with water from a fire hose. Then he was hoisted into the back of a pick-up truck and there was a parade of bread trucks and maintenance trucks around the flight line to the squadron operations building. It would be his moment of glory. We knew that we would receive a less than glorious reception when we returned home to the States.

I knew what was going on back home. My wife Sandy was still attending the university, and she wrote to me on a regular basis and kept me up to date on events at the campus. The university had become a hotbed of anit-war activity. New arrivals to Vietnam reported that newspapers seemed to relish the opportunity to report on these demonstrations—along with the Vietnam body counts. Demonstrators, hippies, counter-culture radicals, and draft dodgers seemed to get a lot of sympathetic media coverage. Returning Vietnam War Veterans were mostly ignored or lambasted for their service.

EC-121 CRASH

I stayed current with newsworthy items in Vietnam by reading the *Stars and Stripes* military newspaper. It documented military events in Vietnam with respectful and unbiased reporting. One article in the March 1970 issue was of special interest. The article reported an event I had witnessed while waiting for takeoff in the arming area. An older four engine propeller-driven Navy EC-121 Super Constellation aircraft was on approach for landing. The EC-121 was sort of an odd shaped transport aircraft, with three vertical tail stabilizers and a dolphin-like arch-shaped fuselage. A civilian version of the aircraft was used as a commercial airliner; it was also the presidential airplane for Dwight Eisenhower. The EC designation meant it was used for electronic intelligence to provide early warning and control of USAF fighter aircraft engaging MIGs. It was the forerunner of airborne early warning and control aircraft that flew orbits over the Gulf of Tonkin and Laos in a search for enemy activity.

Some of my missions intertwined with the intelligence-gathering functions of the EC-121. We dropped cannisters over Laos that exploded in the air and scattered little sensors over the Ho Chi Minh trail. The EC-121 had the capability to monitor enemy movements from those sensor inputs.

This EC-121's approach for landing did not look stable. As it approached the end of the runway, it suddenly started a climb and steep bank to the right as if it were aborting the landing and trying to go around. It rolled up into a ninety-degree banked turn, nosed down, and cartwheeled across the top of an F-4 revetment. I could not believe it; I had just witnessed an aircraft crash. One moment it was an intact airplane. A few seconds later, it was debris scattering across the area. It all happened so fast that it seemed surreal.

Because of the debris, we shut down our F-4 in the arming area and rode back to squadron ops in a maintenance truck. A few days later, the *Stars and Stripes* respectfully reported an accurate description of the accident. Twenty-two Navy airmen lost their lives in that crash, but amazingly there were survivors. The *Stars and Stripes* recounted the thoughts of one survivor who was thrown out of the airplane.

> "The father of three said he was sitting in the extreme end of the aircraft, strapped to the floor next to the door. The tail section of the craft broke away from the main portion of the plane in the crash and that is where most of the nine survivors were reported riding. 'I don't know if I was thrown from the plane or got out myself. I just remember hitting and then being outside, seeing other guys on the ground. I'm not a religious fanatic or anything—but maybe now. I was danged lucky to save my life, there's no doubt about it.'"

I never heard about the cause of the crash. If I were to speculate, Viet Cong were suspected of sitting on a ridgeline just to the west of the approach to that runway. A big slow airplane was an easy target for them. The EC-121 crash was just one of many shocking events during my tour of duty in this war zone. Hopefully, there would not be too many more because the tragedies were starting to wear on me. The rockets, the SAR missions, the pilot losses, the aircraft accidents, the AAA— all this plus the loneliness of being in some god-forsaken part of the world. Even worse, I was putting my rear on the line for an ungrateful country. I had always wanted to be a fighter pilot. I was getting an indoctrination into the real world of being an American fighter pilot.

* * *

Many F-4 aviators appeared to be God fearing people, but few, if any, were so outwardly religious that they pushed their beliefs on anyone. Religious beliefs were generally considered to be a private matter between each individual and their god. Even so, a large plaque that had religious connotations hung in squadron ops. *High Flight* was a sonnet written by John Gillespie Magee, Jr., who was a World War II Royal Canadian Air Force fighter pilot sent to England for combat duty. It is so beautiful that it bears repeating here.

> *Oh, I have slipped the surly bonds of earth,*
> *And danced the skies on laughter-silvered wings;*
> *Sunward I've climbed and joined the tumbling mirth of sun-split*
> *clouds—and done a hundred things You have not dreamed of—*
> *wheeled and soared and swung high in the sunlit silence.*
> *Hovering there I've chased the shouting wind along*
> *and flung my eager craft through footless halls of air.*
> *Up, up the long delirious burning blue*
> *I've topped the wind-swept heights with easy grace,*
> *where never lark, or even eagle, flew;*
> *and, while with silent, lifting mind I've trod*
> *the high untrespassed sanctity of space,*
> *put out my hand and touched the face of God.*

John Gillespie Magee, Jr was killed in 1941 when he was only nineteen years old.

Hanging next to it was a framed aviation picture with a phrase that was partially from Psalm 23:4.

Yea, though I walk through the valley of the shadow of death, I shall fear no evil . . .

It continued with a verse that was not very biblical.

. . . for I am the meanest son of a bitch in the valley.

That persona sort of fit me since I had started my early life as a fearless farm kid thinking I could do no harm, although I was never mean. I spun the tractor around on ice in the driveway, drag-raced my friend, and hung from the top rung of the silo. F-4 pilots showed no outward fear like shaky legs, helium voices, sweats, or twitching eyes. I was good at internalizing my fears with a quietness indicative of a mind feverishly at work. As an F-4 pilot I knew what I was facing. I justified my feelings by thinking: *Bad things only happen to the other guy; I am invincible.*

And when something bad did happen to the other guy: *There, but by the grace of God, go I.* (John Bradford)

This war experience was a thought-provoking time for me. Was this EC-121 airplane crash just one example of a miracle that God worked in some people? For that Navy airman, he worked wonders, while in others he worked the opposite. How would the Lord work in me? Did God have a long-range plan for me or was Vietnam going to be the end of the line? This unpredictability all seemed very troubling.

* * *

There was a chapel on base, so I went to one service during my time in Vietnam. It was a Christmas Eve service. What should have been a joyous occasion was kind of a downer. Back home, I was accustomed to attending a full church on Christmas Eve with family, singing the carols, and then going home to open presents. At this service, there were less than ten people. At the end, a pianist played *Silent Night,* which I considered to be a beautiful hymn. It reminded me of the Christmas Eve services when Dad used to sing it in German. He had a rich baritone voice that harmonized with other older German-speaking men in the congregation. It used to mesmerize me into just wanting to listen. At this service, I tried to sing a few verses, but my lips began to quiver and then tears started, so I had to stop singing for fear that someone would see me. Christmas without my family reminded me that I was in this lonely, depressing place. The thought crossed my mind that there was a possibility that I might never see another Christmas Eve service. That night I prayed my usual prayers and added: *Lord, please let me go back to my family.*

For clarification, I included: *I mean going back to my family alive, and not in a box.*

Rumor had it that some pilots were getting rollbacks on their DEROS. One AC supposedly got a six-month rollback. I was so excited that I wrote to Sandy that I could be coming home early. It was probably not good to get her hopes up especially since the rumor died quickly. It soon became evident that the Air Force policy was that I would be there one year and nothing less.

* * *

I received an urgent message from back home that Grandpa Wick had passed. Sandy and Ma were hoping that I could come home for the funeral. Grandpa was a gentlemanly type of quiet person who carried an aura of respect about him. I spent time with him at his farm during my youth when he was still a farmer, and also a few nights at his house after he moved into town. He appeared to be healthy before I left for Vietnam. Sandy told me that he was walking out to his mailbox on a cold wintry morning and fell to the ground. He possibly died from frozen lungs. Fully expecting the obvious, I asked my commander if I could go home for the funeral. He researched the matter and told me that grandparents were not on the list for an authorized return home due to death. Some stateside ground-pounder had supposedly written a policy that only permitted a return to the States for death of parents, spouse, or children.

A VERY LONG
SAR MISSION

My missions over Laos varied from interdiction, to reconnaissance escort, to MIG cap, to SAR support, to B-52 arc light support—plus whatever else the Air Force needed the F-4s to do. I was sitting on alert at Danang waiting for a call to launch. I had preflighted and cocked my aircraft so that we could launch within five minutes of notification. We got the call to scramble. My AC and I ran to the aircraft, strapped in, fired up the engines, taxied out, and took off. We received priority handling from air traffic controllers and passed up all the other aircraft waiting for takeoff. We were scrambled on a SAR support mission to rescue a downed pilot in the northern part of Laos near the border of North Vietnam. He was down close to Hanoi where the MIGs were based. We carried no bombs, just missiles and the internal gun. Our mission was MIG cap. We were expected to shoot down any MIGs that came near the SAR effort. We orbited for an hour until our fuel got low, hit the tanker, then returned to orbit. We did this again and again and again. Another MIG cap flight replaced us while we refueled.

While sitting on alert, you never knew when or if you were going to scramble. I had been drinking a lot of pop. After doing a couple of those air-to-air refuelings, I had to take a leak. I always stuffed a piddle-pak in my flight suit for that eventuality, but it was anything but high-tech. It was basically a plastic bag with a large neck on it and a sponge inside to absorb the liquid. The engineer who designed it had either not tested it, or else he used a test dummy that had a long hard-on. I might be wrong, but I think it was unlikely that any F-4 pilots flying combat missions were in a frame of mind to inspire a boner so that they could use this gadget. In the small confines of the cockpit, there was no way I could get out of the seat during flight. I had to use this piddle-pak while sitting in the seat. I unhooked my shoulder harness and lap belt just to get at the lower zipper on my flight suit. I reached in to try and find it. It was sort of pinched between my legs, so it required some effort just to locate it. Once I latched onto it, it was obvious that it was not even close to being long enough to reach the neck of that piddle pak. I tried to stretch it out but since I was seated, I could barely get it past the zipper of my flight suit. I had to go bad, so I went. Almost nothing made it into the bag.

In a slow deep monotone voice over guard frequency, there came the following transmission:

"This is Bone Crusher on guard, bogeys, two-zero-one-eight, one-zero-four-one-zero, heading two-one-zero, altitude one-seven-thousand. Bone crusher out."

I looked at my map to confirm that the area represented by these latitude/longitude coordinates was the same area we were orbiting. My head was swiveling back and forth looking for enemy aircraft. I rechecked the radar homing and warning (RHAW) gear to be sure it was tuned and ready. I monitored my radar screen for any sign of a blip. A blip suddenly appeared. Could it be the enemy aircraft (bogeys)? We lit the afterburners and took off in their direction. F-4 pilots relished the opportunity to shoot down a MIG because it was sort of a badge of honor. We knew, or at least we believed, we were flying an aircraft far superior to the MIG.

We had to be careful though, because the MIGs could be suckering us to fly in range of their SAM sites or AAA radar guided guns. The North Vietnamese were cunning; they knew how to lure an unsuspecting pilot into a trap. I knew about their tactics from the intel briefings back at Danang and word of mouth from other pilots. The more you knew about their schemes, the better your chance of survival.

The RHAW gear scope in my cockpit provided indications when an enemy radar was tracking our aircraft. A line emanated from the center of the scope and displayed the relative direction from which the radar signal originated. The line pointed toward the bottom right corner of the scope, so we checked our four o'clock position for a SAM launch. The RHAW system first fed a slow beep-beeping aural signal into my headset. As it detected a stronger enemy radar signal, the aural signal changed to a higher frequency beep-beep. It then changed to a high PRF (pulse recurring frequency), which sounded like a rattlesnake. This indicated that the enemy was now locked on to our aircraft and preparing to launch a SAM.

SAM avoidance was practiced in training. The procedure was developed from the inputs of pilots who flew the Operation Rolling Thunder Campaign over Hanoi in the mid 1960s. The temptation was for a pilot to immediately start evasive maneuvers when first spotting a SAM, but it was not the right decision. The SAM was a highly maneuverable missile that could follow aircraft movements as it closed on the aircraft. The correct procedure for a SAM break required the highest degree of patience. Wait until the missile got within a few hundred feet of the aircraft, then slam the stick forward—much like the spin recovery procedure for the T-37. The aircraft would encounter more than three negative Gs. The missile could not make the rapid transition from its upward vertical trajectory to a negative G downward trajectory, and it disintegrated harmlessly in flight.

SAM launches were not a frequent occurrence in 1970 because all known SAMs were positioned in North Vietnam. President Johnson had restricted US Air Force flights over North Vietnam. We did fly missions close to the North Vietnam border in Laos so SAMs were always a threat. On this mission, we did not observe a SAM launch.

The blip on my radar screen was present for just a few sweeps but then it disappeared. Most likely, the MIGs that approached us had descended to a low altitude where I could not get a distinguishable return from them on my radar. At low altitude, aircraft blended in with ground clutter. We recognized that there was a limit to how far we should pursue a MIG. We could have tried to search for the MIGs at low altitude, but it would have put us within range of numerous ground-based antiaircraft guns. Since these MIGs did not appear to be a threat to the SAR effort, we wisely decided to break off our pursuit and climb back up to our MIG cap altitude.

The downed pilot was successfully rescued. After six long hours of sitting with a wet flight suit, we were finally directed to return to Danang. It was terribly embarrassing after deplaning for this macho fighter pilot to pass by my cohorts with yellow stains on the front of my flight suit.

Another type of mission for us was the reconnaissance escort mission (known as recce escort). It consisted of escorting RF-4s loaded only with high-resolution cameras that photographed enemy storage sites and gun emplacements in North Vietnam. Those pilots flew a vital mission to gather intelligence that could be useful for future targeting. Recce pilots flew at 420 knots, and they had to fly at low altitudes over enemy territory to capture the best pictures. As an escort, we flew slightly above them armed with a full load of ordnance.

It was sort of eerie flying over North Vietnam at those low altitudes knowing there were SAM sites and AAA gun emplacements tracking us that could shoot us down at will. At times, our RHAW gear scope was lit up with strobes from several radar sites tracking us. The North Vietnamese were not interested in attacking us. They obviously read the newspapers from the United States which widely proclaimed that President Johnson had imposed a unilateral bombing halt on North Vietnam. They knew that we were not authorized to bomb them unless one of their trigger-happy NVA gunners fired on our aircraft in which case we were permitted to respond. The North Vietnamese knew better than to solicit the wrath of F-4 pilots.

SOMETHING BIG
ABOUT TO HAPPEN

O n the night prior to May 1, 1970, I was working in the frag shop when a big change to the frag came in from 7th AF Headquarters in Saigon. I knew only that there was a change but was not permitted access to any of the details. It was a top-secret frag, with access restricted to a limited number of people at Danang. Bits and pieces of the change were disseminated to various units on a need-to-know basis. Squadrons were advised to schedule pilots for four-ship flights. Briefing times were posted on the squadron scheduling board with no mission specifics. Maintenance personnel were advised to get four aircraft ready for each of the scheduled takeoff times. Munitions personnel were advised to upload the aircraft with different ordnance loads. Tower controllers were advised that they needed to keep taxiways clear of all other aircraft. Four-ship formations of F-4s would need to depart at precise takeoff times. Pilots were locked out of intel, so we sensed that something big was about to happen. I was scheduled to fly on the first mission and soon learned that the missions were a well-kept secret for a good reason.

I was paired to fly with my favorite AC. I found him to be an interesting person who shared my character traits as easy going and unexcitable. He was thin and sort of scraggly looking with his flight suit hanging on him. We had previously flown several missions together and worked great as a team. He did his thing up front and he let me do my thing in the back. Both of us recognized that our primary objective was to survive and get back home.

We were not going to change the course of the war with just our missions. He let me film one mission with my Super 8 movie camera while he did the refueling and bomb run. On another mission, he let me do the roll-in on the target. I did not have a pipper in the back so I just kind of pointed the nose of the aircraft at the target. He called out the altitudes and pickled the bombs. I flew the escape maneuver. In Laos, it did not matter if bombs were a little off target since the eastern half of Laos consisted of numerous Ho Chi Minh trail targets.

My AC and I smoked and drank, swore, and had many laughs and stories to share at the squadron bar over a few beers. One difference between the two of us was that I was an occasional smoker whereas he was a chain smoker who was usually seen with a cigarette hanging out of his mouth.

F-4 pilots always wore oxygen masks while flying. An oxygen regulator in the aircraft regulated the amount of oxygen pilots received based on the cabin altitude. At lower altitude, pilots got a regulated amount of oxygen mixed with ambient air, and at higher cabin altitudes, pilots got 100 percent oxygen. There was always some residual oxygen floating around the masks, even when the regulator was turned off. After our last bombing pass, my AC would tell me: "You got it, I'm off."

It meant that I had control of both the aircraft and the radio transmissions. He unfastened his oxygen mask from one side of his helmet. He had easy access to the pack of cigarettes in a zipper pocket on the upper left sleeve of his flight suit. Oxygen was highly flammable. The first time he pulled out a cigarette and lit it, I thought for sure we were going to blow up. I never expressed my concerns to him so that sort of meant that it was acceptable to me. It cemented our friendship and trust in each other, and we never blew up.

I was happy to be flying with my favorite AC on this super-secret mission. We met at squadron ops to put on our G suit, life vest, and gun holster. We carried our helmet bag that contained our helmet and checklists and walked over to intel together.

My AC knew that I worked in the frag shop and thought that I might have some inside information. "Any idea where we are going today?" he asked.

"Nope, not a clue."

There was some speculation about possibly going into Cambodia. President Nixon had hinted that he was going to clean out the North Vietnamese sanctuary areas across the border from South Vietnam in Cambodia. It was sort of a secret to the media back home, but the US had been conducting raids into Cambodia for several weeks, so Nixon would only be revealing something that had been going on for quite some time.

Maybe it was going to be some mass gaggle into Laos. Bombing Laos was a regular occurrence and an unkept secret, so it did not make sense to now do a super-secret mission to Laos.

Going back to North Vietnam was a possibility but it would be politically risky. If word got out that Nixon restarted the bombing of North Vietnam, the anti-war protesters would be reignited with their hate-filled rhetoric. The United States military would be escalating the Vietnam War at a time when the American body count was already high. Those terrible United States Air Force pilots would be bombing innocent North Vietnamese women and children.

Eight of us pilots for the first of those super-secret missions walked into intel and were handed a folder with all the maps, targets, TOTs (time over target), taxi times, takeoff times, ordnance and whatever else needed to be known about the mission. Normally, each pilot had to prepare their own maps, but everything had been neatly prepared for us.

We were going back over North Vietnam as the first wave of a massive assault on NVA storage areas. Our target was the triple A (antiaircraft artillery) sites surrounding a supply depot near the coastal city of Vinh, North Vietnam, about 465 kilometers north of Danang. From the RF-4 reconnaissance data, the area was known to be a major storage depot for NVA war supplies. It was heavily defended by AAA and SAMS. The ordnance load for our four aircraft was wall-to-wall cluster bombs, also known as CBUs. Timed-release bomblets from the CBUs would keep the gunners *heads down* for about thirty minutes or longer, to enable strike aircraft to drop their Mk-82 bombs on the storage depots. All the missions for this day were sequenced with precise TOTs. Every flyable F-4 at Danang was utilized in this North Vietnam bombing operation. F-4s from other bases in Vietnam and Thailand were also tasked for these missions and the exact timing of the TOTs (time over targets) was necessary to ensure there were no conflicting missions over the target at the same time.

It was an exciting change in the direction of the war that the United States Air Force was going back to bomb North Vietnam. It had been ridiculous that President Johnson had ordered the bombing halt. That halt had allowed the NVA to safely stockpile wartime supplies just across the border. Wars ought to be fought on enemy territory. South Vietnam, Laos, and Cambodia were not the enemy. The enemy was North Vietnam, and it was the communist regime from North Vietnam that tried to overrun South Vietnam and spread their evil doctrine throughout Southeast Asia. The NVA were the ones that trained the Viet Cong in South Vietnam and supplied them with weapons. Nixon had the courage to permit the military to take the war to the enemy's turf. I applauded his decision and was enthused to be a part of this new direction in the war.

Pilots in the 366 TFW were excited to take part in these missions. For one pilot, it would not happen. He was relegated to desk duty because he was DNIF (pronounced da-nif). DNIF meant duty not including flying. He could do desk duty, but he could not fly an airplane. He was DNIF because he evidently did not pay attention to one of the briefings at jungle survival school in the Philippines. Air Force medical personnel had briefed pilots on the potential dangers of sex with Southeast Asian women: you could get more than you bargained for. They described cases of venereal disease where patients had to be flown from Vietnam to the Philippines for treatment. Some would be staying in the Philippines well past their DEROS. One disease they described was elephantiasis which was an enlargement of the testicles. It was possibly caused by sex, although the cause was open to debate. In any case, grotesque pictures of elephantiasis were shown during the briefing for maximum shock effect.

This DNIF pilot had been on a *good deal* aircraft delivery trip to Okinawa where an F-4 repair facility was located. Pilots flew an F-4 there, left the aircraft, overnighted, and then came back to Danang the next day with a different repaired aircraft. The overnight in Okinawa offered temptations to a horny pilot. This fellow was single and thought it was okay to recruit one of the pretty locals for his overnight pleasure.

He did not get elephantiasis; but he did get the clap. Clap was also known as the drips, or a more medically appropriate name, gonorrhea. Rumor had it that it was called the clap because it hurt so bad when you tried to pee that when it finally came, you clapped for joy. This pilot had to go to the doctor, who gave him penicillin shots which caused him to be grounded. He had to sit behind a desk and watch as his comrades paraded to intel one after another for one of the most interesting missions of their tour. Even worse, he had to take a lot of ribbing. At that time a politically correct culture had not yet been invented. Even if it were, it probably would not have made any difference in the middle of a war zone.

Guys clapped when they walked by him. When discussing a mission with him, we interjected a comment that there was a *drip, drip, drip* of information. One pilot asked him: "On Asian girls, does it run north and south, or east and west?"

He took it all in good spirit.

I had been on one of these good deal trips to Okinawa. But I had a mama back home waiting for me and was committed to being loyal to her. I did not want to take anything bad from Southeast Asia back to her.

* * *

A four-ship mission was somewhat unusual at Danang since most other missions were two-ship. We would be number three in a four-ship flight which was the preferred position. We were happy to not be in the lead because lead had all the responsibility of getting the formation to and from the target. All three had to do was follow lead and keep up with the frequency changes.

"Gunfighter Two-One flight, go channel four."

"Twoop," "Threep," "Four."

"Gunfighter Two-One flight check in."

"Twoop," "Threep . . ."

There was frustration in lead's voice.

"Four, you up?"

When a formation wingman did not answer, lead had to try to find out what frequency he was on. It detracted from their concentration on mission essentials. Lead had a couple of options to get him on the correct frequency. He could go back to the previous frequency to see if he were still there. If it occurred in flight, he could wag his wings to get the wingman's attention. Then lead would hold up an appropriate number of fingers next to his helmet so that the wingman could see them. For anything greater than five, he would first make a fist and then display the appropriate number of fingers. For example, seven would be a fist followed by two fingers. A third option for lead would be to transmit the new frequency on the guard frequency of 243.0, which all aircraft monitored. This was sort of a last resort because lead would be broadcasting to anyone listening that his wingman was not paying attention to frequency changes.

If an aircraft were not up on frequency it could also be the result of radio failure. If it happened on the ground, the wingman would be forced to abort the mission; if already airborne, he would fly the mission as planned. Radio failure procedures during flight was a prebriefed item. That wingman would still roll in on the target according to the prebriefed sequence of bombing passes, but the other three aircraft in the formation would need to constantly be aware of his location to prevent any mishaps.

Four must have recognized that at this point in the taxi to the end of the runway, he should be on tower frequency: "Four's up."

Two minutes before takeoff time, our flight of four F-4s was cleared onto the runway. We did our engine run-ups to ensure engine performance was satisfactory. I looked back at the taxiway leading to the runway and there was almost a mile-long line of F-4s waiting for their precise takeoff time. What a sight to see all those beastly-looking aircraft painted with shark's teeth on the nose, fully loaded with bombs destined to obliterate some part of North Vietnam. At the precise time to the second, lead started his takeoff roll; ten seconds later another, and then us. F-4s always took off single ship because the heavy ordnance load restricted lead from giving up any power just so the wingman could stay in position for a formation takeoff. F-4s needed every available pound of thrust to get airborne, so on takeoff maximum afterburner power was used. Our staged afterburner lit off. To any outside observer it created a deafening roar. An F-4 accelerating down the runway caused the ground to rumble. A long stream of fire spewed out the rear of the aircraft. Another F-4 formation would be taking off from Danang after a five-minute interval, creating the same aural turmoil. It had to be obvious to any outside observer at Danang that something special was happening that day.

The thundering sounds of all those F-4s taking off in exacting sequence had to arouse the curiosity of anyone on base. In the intelligence briefing, we were informed that there was a reason that this mission was super-secret and why we could not talk to any outsider about it. There were probably reporters snooping around trying to get that big scoop on a story so that they could reveal it to *the world*. Reporters did not garner much respect from F-4 pilots when they did not honor our safety.

We attained our liftoff speed at 190 knots. Lead started a slow turn to the left to shorten the closure distance so wingmen could join up in formation. Aircraft were positioned in finger four formation much like the four fingers on a person's hand minus the thumb. Lead was the middle finger; two was on the left wing; three on the right wing; and four flew off three's right wing. Three was the preferred position because of the location of the controls in the cockpit. F-4 pilots always flew with their right hand on the stick and their left hand on the throttle, so it was most natural to look to the left.

Once the gear was retracted, my AC turned over control of the aircraft to me. I had flown enough formation rejoins that I could expeditiously slide into position on lead's wing without jockeying back and forth. Even though the number four pilot tried, my ego would not let him join up on my wing before I got into position on lead's wing. It would be a reflection on my piloting skill. Once I joined up, four had to hope that I was steady on the controls. If three was bobbing up and down to stay in position, then four also bobbed up and down but at an accentuated rate. Flying four was especially challenging when going through an area of turbulence when all the aircraft in the formation were bobbing around.

I quickly slid into position, placing my cockpit about five feet from lead's wingtip. It was important to stay close so that I would not lose sight of lead in case we flew into dense clouds. Breaking out of formation because of losing sight of lead was generally a sign of poor airmanship. F-4 pilots took a lot of pride in their flying abilities.

The target in North Vietnam was a relatively short flying distance from Danang. Due to its proximity, our flight would not refuel for this mission. A tanker was orbiting over the Gulf of Tonkin just in case we ran low after our bomb runs. Lead established an orbit over the target at 15,000 feet until each aircraft reported a visual on the target. There was no FAC; we had to find the target ourselves. It was easy to identify because paved roads led us directly to it.

Lead rolled out of the formation first.

"Lead's in."

Two proceeded a little further around in the orbit so he would not be following the same flight path as lead in case some NVA gunner was zeroing in on lead. A short time later,

"Two's in."

We were up next.

"Three's in."

We appeared to be successful at surprising the North Vietnamese on the first pass. Perhaps the gunners were sleeping on the job, or maybe they thought the F-4s were there to take pictures like the RF-4s did on their recce missions. For the second pass though, the gunners were awake after they probably realized that this was a real bombing mission. There were lots of them.

My head was on a swivel, expecting this response from the NVA. I could see numerous gunfire bursts on the ground and tracers rising in the air. One gunner zeroed in on our aircraft. Normally in the daytime we could only see the tracers from our cockpit. This time, the bullets were so close that I could also see the red fiery bullets between the tracers, and they were closing on our aircraft. I yelled to my AC,

"Jink! Jink! Jink!"

My yell alarmed the AC, and he reacted to the intensity in my voice. He sucked the stick back; then violently slammed it forward to destroy the tracking solution of the gunner. The G meter in the cockpit had three needles. One pointer gave continuous G readings; the other two gave maximum positive and negative Gs encountered during flight. Our maximum positive reading exceeded 8.5 Gs and negative readings exceeded -3 Gs, which pegged the needles at their limits.

The cockpit was eerily quiet on the way back to Danang. It got me thinking that some higher authority had to have prevented almost certain destruction of our aircraft. My AC smoked a couple of cigarettes, maybe even three or four, as I flew the aircraft back to Danang.

Flying the F-4 required little muscular strength. Manipulation of the controls involved slight wrist movements to control the stick and a slight arm movement to control the throttle. The G forces and rapid tossing of my body back and forth in the cockpit was equivalent to any physically challenging workout. The stressors exhausted my mental stamina. I was physically and mentally drained. My flight suit was soaked with sweat. I stepped down from the ladder to the tarmac after deplaning, and I needed to pause for a moment at the bottom to be sure that there was still enough strength in my legs to walk.

F-4s from bases in the northern part of South Vietnam and Thailand were all involved in this coordinated bombing campaign against North Vietnam. There were several F-4 missions dedicated to this two-day campaign and the results were good. Strike pilots reported seeing many secondary explosions. Equally important, those missions sent a message to the North Vietnamese that they could no longer safely sit behind their border. They now had to worry about Americans dropping bombs on their heads in their home territory.

After the two days of bombing North Vietnam, it was back to Laos. I was accustomed to flying missions in Laos and had flown over one hundred missions half-way through my tour in Vietnam. Not all missions were the hair-raising type. Most were sort of routine, if there was such a thing, but those were quickly forgotten. The not-so-routine missions were the ones that would be cemented into my mind forever.

Most Laos missions consisted of bombing the Ho Chi Minh trail with 500-pound bombs or CBUs, but there were some variations. The Air Force experimented with new technology during the war. Laser-guided 500-pound bombs required two aircraft for the drop. One aircraft dropped the bomb in the vicinity of the laser beam; the other aircraft used the laser beam to guide it to its target.

We tested launching guided rockets to destroy targets hidden in caves. GIBs pointed the aircraft toward the target. The AC launched the rocket toward the cave. While the GIB continued to fly a shallow descent toward the target, the AC used a joystick in the cockpit to send signals to the rocket to direct it into the cave. It worked okay, but there were not a lot of easily identifiable targets in caves.

TEST FLIGHT
TO/FROM HELL

Ineeded a change from flying just tactical bombing missions, so I volunteered for another duty to fly maintenance test flights. F-4s that had been through a major maintenance procedure required a test flight to verify airborne operation of propulsion (engines), air conditioning, pressurization, hydraulics, flight controls, landing gear, electrical, and avionics systems before the aircraft could be released to fly a tactical mission.

Aircraft that had undergone an engine change required a high-speed run to verify that the aircraft engines had adequate power to attain a speed of Mach two. To get to Mach two we had to find the coldest temperatures in the atmosphere where jet engines performed at their peak. The coldest temperatures were normally found in the tropopause, which is the atmospheric layer between the troposphere and the stratosphere. The tropopause is an atmospheric layer in which the air temperature remains constant throughout its thickness. It varies in altitude from 30,000 feet to 50,000 feet above the ground. Before our test flight, I checked the weather maps to locate the height and thickness of the tropopause for our high-speed run.

Once airborne after all our low altitude checks were completed, we climbed to 35,000 feet to prepare for our high-speed run. The temperature at 35,000 feet was minus fifty-six degrees Celsius (minus sixty-eight degrees Fahrenheit) so the speed of sound was 660 mph or 574 knots. We needed to go twice that fast, or faster than the speed of most bullets, in order to qualify the engines.

We flew a stripped-down F-4 that did not have an external fuel tank nor pylons attached to the wings. We started the high-speed run just short of the Chinese border heading back toward Danang. Mach two required full afterburner, so we would burn through a lot of fuel, and we wanted to be close to Danang when we got low on fuel. After achieving Mach two, we eased the F-4 into a slow climb to ensure that a sudden aircraft attitude change would not cause the engines to compressor stall and flameout due to a change of airflow through them. If we lost engine power, there would be no cabin pressurization and our time of useful consciousness would be less than nine seconds. The climb to 50,000 feet enabled us to bleed off airspeed and to check the pressurization system. We then coasted into Danang at idle power for landing.

I usually met the AC at the aircraft. On one mission, he was acting a little strange. I was somewhat suspicious, but not to the point where I would say anything to him. During the before engine start checks, his responses to the checklist were somewhat imprecise. After engine start, he asked me to control the throttles while he steered as we taxied to the runway. He struggled to keep the F-4 centered on the yellow taxiway line. He told me to do the takeoff which was unusual but somewhat exciting for me since I had limited visibility forward from the back seat. I used differential braking to steer the aircraft down the runway until airflow made the rudders effective for directional control. After airborne, I called for "Gear up."

Nothing happened. The F-4 gear handle was only installed in the front cockpit so I had no way to retract the gear. In a firmer voice, I again called for: "Gear up."

The gear still did not retract. It was impossible to do all the required checks for an FCF (functional check flight) with the gear down. The AC asked the tower controller for permission to fly around in the local area to burn off fuel. I thought it would be most prudent to just go back to Danang and land. Fuel load was not an issue of whether we could land or not. I was starting to get a little suspicious of his actions and wondered if he had even raised the gear handle. He then commanded: "I have the aircraft."

We were orbiting in the approach corridor to runway one seven at Danang. The corridor was normally very congested with airplanes on approach to landing at Danang. Danang was the busiest airport in the world, with over 2,500 air operations daily. Our flight path was unpredictable, so tower controllers asked us several times:

"Gunfighter Two-One test flight, what are your intentions?"

He was flying high G turns, rapid climbs and steep dives. I did not know what to say and got very alarmed when he asked me: "Ever done an aileron roll in an F-4?"

I had done a lot of aileron rolls in pilot training in the T-37 and T-38, but I had never done one in an F-4 with the gear down at this low altitude.

He started the roll from a flat pitch attitude. Normally, if somebody was going to do an aileron roll, they first got the nose of the aircraft pointed upward. He rolled the airplane over to a ninety-degree bank angle and the nose started to drop below the horizon. We were destined to do a split S straight into the ground. He recognized his dilemma and rolled the airplane back to level flight.

I had enough, so I demanded that we go back to Danang and land. This guy was slurring his speech and acting like someone who was inebriated. Either he had been drinking a significant amount before takeoff and I was oblivious to it, or he had a bottle stashed in his flight suit and was swigging from it during flight. Flight suits had zippered pockets on the lower legs, so it would have been easy to shove a pint bottle of booze in it and take a swig during flight. Alcohol has a stronger effect on the body at higher altitudes than at sea level. Higher altitudes have reduced atmospheric pressure on the body. The lesser pressure reduces the ability of the hemoglobin in the blood to absorb oxygen. Lower oxygen levels at higher altitudes impairs the ability of the body to metabolize alcohol, leading to quicker absorption of alcohol in the body and enhanced intoxication. When our flight ascended, the alcohol had an increasingly pronounced effect.

I was desperately trying to convince him to get our aircraft back on the ground. We had exceeded the landing gear speed limit. The landing gear doors were not designed to withstand high G forces and could easily be damaged, or even ripped off if speed or G limits were exceeded. The high G maneuvering with the landing gear down could be affecting the overall integrity of the aircraft. I was concerned about whether we had a structurally sound aircraft for a safe landing.

This AC was not ready to land, and I became part of his captive audience of one.

"You see that radar dome?"

I did not answer him. Of course, I saw that radar dome; it was easily visible out in the distance. I had flown past it on many occasions because it was located on Monkey Mountain, just a few miles from Danang to the east of the approach to runway one seven. What was this guy thinking of now?

"I am going to roll the tires across that dome"

You gotta be shittin' me.

He turned our F-4 and headed straight for that radar dome. We were rapidly closing on it at an airspeed of 300 knots, which was far in excess of the maximum gear down speed of 250 knots. Plus, we were now flying at an altitude below the top of this radar dome. In a firm voice, I commanded: "Pull up!"

No response.

We were going to crash into that dome. With my left hand, I grabbed the ejection seat handle between my legs; and with my right hand, I pulled back on the stick with all my might. I could feel him trying to resist me on the stick. We were no longer two F-4 pilots working as a crew, but two individual pilots with opposing objectives. His objective was to perform a stupid stunt; mine was to survive. My mind was racing. I had to decide within an instant whether to stay with the aircraft or punch out. I knew that if I punched out, he was going to crash, so I took a chance. Evidently, my pull on the stick was strong enough that we cleared the dome. After several combat missions, this was the first time I had placed my hand on that ejection seat handle with the intent of using it.

My method of thwarting his plans was evidently enough to bring him to his senses. He must have recognized that he was incapable of landing the aircraft.

"George, take the airplane, let's go back and land."

After we got back to Danang, the crew chief probably sensed something was not right when I threw off my shoulder straps and stormed out of the aircraft without saying a word nor waiting for the AC. I was upset. I strutted to squadron ops, flung off my flying gear, and proceeded directly to my room to spend some time contemplating about how close I had come to dying because of this stupid stunt. I was mostly upset with myself for not recognizing the gravity of that situation sooner. It nearly cost me my life. Had I confronted him while we were still on the ground before flight, this disastrous flight could have been avoided. Some other GIBs saw that I was upset and stopped by my room to ask me what happened. I let it all out. It had been a terrible experience and it was good to get it out of my system.

After hearing about my frightening ordeal, all the GIBs resolved to never fly with this AC. He got the message. He was a short-timer, so he was going home soon. I attended the going away party. After dinner and a few drinks, honorees were offered the opportunity to make a few comments. He walked up to the microphone and I could not believe what I heard.

"I would like to acknowledge one person here tonight for whom I have the highest admiration and respect. He is truly a professional pilot. I want to publicly thank Lt. George Kohn for saving my life."

When he finished his brief speech, he walked over to my table and gave me a big hug. No further explanations were necessary. It was quite heartwarming to have been singled out for appreciation from someone who recognized that he had made a huge error in judgement. It took a big, big man to acknowledge this mistake. Yes, F-4 pilots were fallible.

R&R FINALLY

ir Force members in Vietnam were offered a period of R&R (rest and relaxation) and I desperately needed a break away from the war. The two most popular spots for R&R were Hawaii and Australia. Single guys went to the very friendly country of Australia; married guys met their sweethearts in the equally friendly state of Hawaii. There was a reserved airline seat available to either of those destinations.

Sandy arranged to meet me in Hawaii along with our five-year old son, Paul. They arrived first in Honolulu, where they were showered with cordiality by Army personnel from Fort DeRussy. An Army chaplain briefed the wives.

"Do not expect to see the same person as the one who left you back home. Your spouse will be a changed person. War changes people. Do not ask them about any of their experiences in combat. They need to get away from that war for a while. It is okay to talk about things back home. They will want to hear about you and the family. Give them lots of love, and most importantly, have a good time."

My flight landed at Hickam Air Base in Hawaii and I was bused over to Fort DeRussy to meet Sandy and Paul. We quickly spotted each other and ran into a big hug, then it was off to find a place to stay. The Outrigger Hotel offered reasonably priced accommodations for military personnel, plus it was directly located on the beautiful Waikiki beach. I could not wait to get to the room after the long flight, and especially after a long time away from my beautiful wife and son. It was a heartwarming moment when my son jumped up on my lap and gave me a big hug as a sign of how much he loved and missed me. During our short week together, we walked the beach, went to a luau, and listened to Don Ho sing *Tiny Bubbles*. Don Ho showed the highest respect toward military personnel, especially those on R&R from Vietnam. He asked us to stand during his show while the audience gave us a long applause. The Hawaiian people showered us with cordiality. It was a welcome respite from the hatred of the Vietnam War.

It did not take long for reality to set in that I would have to leave beautiful Hawaii and go back to Danang. There was some consolation in the fact that I was now over the hump by passing the halfway point in my tour of duty in Vietnam. At least now, the countdown did not seem quite as ominous as when I first got there back in November.

CAMBODIA—NO RETURN

May through September was the wet season in Laos, so the Ho Chi Minh trails were not easily traversable by the NVA. Since they could not drive their trucks down the dirt trails, they resorted to bicycles, oxcarts, and human pack animals to haul their supplies. The Air Force F-4 interdiction campaign over Laos came to a near standstill. The bombing campaign transitioned to targets in South Vietnam and Cambodia. The air war in South Vietnam consisted mostly of providing close air support to friendly ground forces. In Cambodia, it consisted of cleaning out staging areas that were used by the NVA to stockpile their wartime supplies.

To the public back home, Cambodia was supposedly off-limits. On April 30th, the day before our mission over North Vietnam, President Nixon announced that the US was going to clean out those storage sites in Cambodia. F-4 air operations into Cambodia had already been going on for several days, perhaps even weeks, but the announcement served as an effective ploy to divert media attention from the North Vietnam bombing campaign.

Cambodia was a beautiful country, with acres upon acres of pristine rubber tree plantations. The terrain was relatively flat. It was a welcome change from the scenery of the mountainous, densely vegetated jungle topography in eastern Laos. The AAA threat in Cambodia came from the highly mobile 23mm guns and small arms gunfire. Our F-4 bombing tactics changed to low-altitude, low-angle delivery, which enabled more precise placement of bombs on target.

I was assigned to fly a Cambodia mission on June 18, 1970 with an AC who I did not particularly like to fly with. He always seemed to press below the pickle altitude. I would tell him to pull up, but he would keep on pressing. It got to the point where I no longer told him to pull up, I just pulled back on the stick whenever we reached pickle altitude. It ticked him off because it threw our bombs long and off target. I did not care because ACs were not supposed to press, and GIBs were instructed to pull back on the stick if they did. Besides, it was my butt that was on the line.

This Cambodia mission was a two-ship formation with us in the lead. Our wingman front seater was Major Harry McLamb, who was nicknamed *Hoss*. If he had been permitted to wear a ten-gallon cowboy hat, he would possibly have resembled Hoss Cartwright in the television series *Bonanza*. The back-seater was Major Carl Drake. He appeared to be a somewhat subdued navigator. I did not know much about him, because I do not remember drinking beer or socializing with him. I think that the first time I met him was in the briefing room for this mission.

Our mission to Cambodia started out as routine. The FAC identified the target; my AC and I rolled in and pickled our 500 pounders. We bottomed out of our descent a couple hundred feet above the ground. After both aircrews finished dropping their bombs, the FAC asked if we had guns. FACs knew the capabilities of the F-4 since they worked with them on a regular basis, but they did not know which model of F-4 we were flying. Some Gunfighter flights were D models, which did not have internal guns, and some were E models, which did have the internal 20mm gun.

I responded, "Affirmative, we have guns."

"I just spotted a truck parked in an open area. I am putting down a smoke. When you have the smoke in sight, you are cleared in."

We were orbiting over the target at 10,000 feet and it was easy to spot the smoke amid the sparsely vegetated Cambodian landscape. My AC armed our 20mm gun. I slid my thumb toward the radio transmit button to advise our wingman that we were in on the target. I was just getting ready to transmit, when he announced:

"Two's in."

We broke off our run-in and climbed back to 10,000 feet. I watched two conduct his run-in. There were puffs of smoke from his blazing gun, but then, almost instantaneously, the scene took on a bad appearance. What once was an airplane firing a blazing gun immediately turned into disintegrating pieces of debris and the sickening sight of a huge fireball. F-4 debris was strewn across the ground. The FAC also saw it, and he flew over the site to confirm the obvious. They had crashed.

The flight back to Danang seemed to take an eternity. The discussion between my AC and I mostly centered on how that could have happened.

Maybe the AC took a hit to the cockpit that incapacitated him and there was insufficient reaction time for the GIB to recover the aircraft. Possibly, the aircrew became fixated on strafing the target and lost track of their minimum strafing altitude. The 1,000-foot minimum altitude applied to strafing runs as well as bombing runs. An F-4 in a ten-degree descent at 500 knots lost considerable altitude before dishing out at the bottom. There was a very narrow margin for error. Or, they may have been distracted by ground fire from AAA and descended too low to safely recover.

During our long, somber flight back to Danang as a single ship, the FAC briefed us on his observations of the crash site. He had watched the entire scenario and confirmed that there were no parachutes to indicate that either crewmember had ejected; there was zero chance the crew survived. But what he also saw was interesting. The target was not an actual truck but the plywood mock-up of a truck. The enemy had set up a trap with a contingent of enemy marksmen with small arms and camouflaged antiaircraft guns next to the trap. The enemy was ready and waiting for us.

After landing, we were met at the aircraft by the wing commander, who escorted us to his office in the wing headquarters building. Since I had observed the entire scenario, he asked me to describe everything in exacting detail.

"Did you see any chutes?"

"No sir."

"Was there any chance that either or both of them survived?"

"No sir. There was zero chance."

I knew why he was asking these questions. The wing commander would have to send a letter of condolence to the next of kin for both the men. The content of the letter would be copied from a standard template into which he just needed to insert the names.

"It is with deepest regret that I inform you that [*name*] has been killed in combat."

Back in the States, an Air Force officer in a class A blue uniform, accompanied by a military chaplain, would knock on the door of the next of kin. They did not have to say a word for a wife to know the grim nature of their visit.

"On behalf of the secretary and the chief of staff of the United States Air Force, I regret to inform you that your husband died in combat."

It had been a shocking scene to see this F-4 disintegrate right before my eyes. It was hard to comprehend how, in a split second, two lives could suddenly be snuffed out.

The colonel asked, "Lt. Kohn, how are you doing? Do you want to stand down for a few days?"

I did not want to sit around and think about it. It was especially difficult to justify in my mind why we were not the first ones to roll in on that target. It was best to immediately get back to flying, because the more I thought about it, the worse it could be on my mental state.

"No sir, I would prefer to keep flying."

I volunteered to fly a combat mission the next day.

The official account of this tragedy differs slightly from my recollection. The scene of that disintegrating F-4 is vividly engrained in my memory. In any case, my deepest belated condolences to the families of those heroic wingmen who sacrificed their lives for me.

ON BASE DRAMA

A bunch of GIBs were sitting around in my room listening to music from the stereo system when one of them asked offhandedly: "Did you hear about the latest incident on base?"

The other pilots shook their heads, indicating that nobody had heard about anything too dramatic other than the normal course of events at Danang.

"They shot a gook who was up on the water tower," he said.

A Viet Cong was up there trying to dump poison in the water. VC did not wear military uniforms or exhibit features different from anyone else in the local populace. There were many Vietnamese locals employed at Danang who had unlimited access to the base.

Another GIB walked into the room.

"Y'all want to see something that should be interesting?"

F-4 pilots came from different parts of the United States, so it was not difficult to suspect from his southern drawl that this fellow was from Mississippi.

"A Navy A-4 Skyhawk is flying around in the pattern with a landing gear problem."

The A-4 was a smaller, single-seat jet fighter aircraft. It would normally return to its aircraft carrier for landing, but the Navy did not want him because if he crashed, it would foul their deck. Instead, they diverted him to Danang.

We ran out to the flight line to watch. The A-4 pilot made a flyby so the tower controllers could confirm that one of the main landing gear was not down. Marines on the other side of the runway controlled fire/rescue at Danang. Their big fire trucks sprayed a strip of foam on the runway to minimize the potential for fire. The A-4 pilot touched down perfectly in the middle of the foam. He held the wing up as long as possible until insufficient lift over the wing caused it to eventually drag on the runway. Sparks flew out from under the aircraft. The pilot got the aircraft stopped directly in front of our viewing area. He did an immediate egress and ran the equivalent of an Olympic sprint to a safe location moments before ammo on the aircraft started exploding. The Marine firefighters moved quickly into the midst of ammo popping off and they doused the aircraft with foam to prevent damage to nearby structures. It was an amazing display of courage.

LETTERS TO AND
FROM HOME

S andy wrote to me every week, and I read every letter over and over. I wrote to Sandy maybe once a month and to Ma only once during my entire tour in Vietnam. It was certainly not frequent enough, but I did not have much to write home about. I could not write about my missions, because they were classified, or the rocket attacks at Danang, as that would be alarming to them. As for good things to say about Danang or the Vietnam War, well, uh, uh, maybe there was something, but I could not think of anything. I received a thick packet of letters from Mary, a friend of Sandy's who was a Pennsylvania grade school English teacher. She had each of her students write a personal letter to me. I considered their letters thoughtful and heartwarming, but it bothered me that I could not formulate the right words to return their nice gesture.

One letter from Sandy in August of 1970 was somewhat depressing. There was a bombing at the University of Wisconsin, where I had gone to school. The bombers were anti-war demonstrators. One person inside the building was killed. That bombing gave me a feeling of worthlessness for everything I was doing in Vietnam. I thought that I, along with others, were putting our rear ends on the line so that all Americans could enjoy our cherished freedoms to live in peace.

I was sitting in the arming area waiting for takeoff on August 17, 1970. In the distance, a large fireball lit up the sky. We took off and flew our mission. After returning, I was notified that the fireball was the result of a crash in which Steve Melnick, a friend from F-4 training in California, was killed. It occurred about ten miles south of Danang during a night strike mission. He was flying as an instructor in the back seat of the lead aircraft. There were two different accounts of what happened. One was that his flight encountered hostile antiaircraft fire. The other was that the two Phantoms collided in midair.

There was a third account that was rumored among pilots at Danang, which seemed to be the most plausible. It was nighttime and there was a solid undercast cloud layer. To find the target, they needed to descend through the cloud deck. The bottom of the cloud deck was at a low altitude obscuring tall mountain peaks. Captain Melnick and his trainees were possibly distracted by enemy gunfire. When bullets were flying, they lost focus on a mountain peak up ahead. Both aircraft flew into the mountain in formation with the loss of all four crewmembers. It was possibly the most difficult letter I had to write to inform Sandy of this tragic loss.

MISSIONS GALORE

The Cambodia operations ended soon because the storage areas were cleaned out, leaving few remaining targets. There were occasional missions over Laos, but they did not entail dive bombings. The F-4 had the capability to drop bombs somewhere near a target from an altitude of 25,000 feet. There was relatively little enemy resistance at that altitude, although an occasional tracer would pop up through the clouds. It was sort of a long shot that the enemy could hit us up there. If they did fire, maybe they were just training a new gunner.

I programmed the coordinates for our target into our inertial navigation system. The F-4 computer used a predetermined trajectory to calculate the correct parameters for releasing the bombs. Its accuracy was questionable. We joked that there were probably a lot of ticked-off monkeys in Laos.

* * *

The B-52 was affectionately known by the acronym BUFF or Big Ugly Fat Fellow as the media politely referred to them. In Vietnam, the last *F* in BUFF had another designation not to be mentioned in public. B-52s were huge four-engine bombers with a wingspan of 185 feet and a maximum takeoff weight of 488,000 pounds. Each B-52 could haul more than one hundred 500-pound bombs. The pockmarked landscape provided visual evidence of where they had carpet-bombed. The DMZ was a frequent target to stem the flow of enemy supplies from the North into South Vietnam.

A couple of my missions were tasked to escort B-52s. It was sort of a joke. I rarely saw the B-52s. We loitered in the general area, making sure we were not anywhere near them when they released their bombs. Supposedly, we were there to provide cover in case of an airborne attack, but the MIGs were confined to the Hanoi area. The B-52s were a sitting duck for SAMs but F-4s could not do anything to prevent a SAM attack against them.

F-4 pilots carried on a friendly banter about BUFF pilots that was intended to be all in fun. We joked that they dropped their bombs from outer space and still got mission counters. To be honest, BUFF drivers flying those huge monsters over Laos and North Vietnam amid intense enemy resistance were equally as heroic as any other pilot.

B-52s were tasked to intensively bomb North Vietnam during the eleven-day Linebacker II operation in December of 1972. More than 200 B-52s dropped 15,000 tons of bombs on targets in Hanoi and Haiphong. Fifteen B-52s were lost mostly due to SAMs; twenty-six crewmembers were recovered, twenty-five came up missing in action, thirty-three became prisoners of war, and eight were either killed in action or later died of wounds. The Linebacker II campaign brought the North Vietnamese to the negotiating table. The Paris Peace Accord was signed in January of 1973. Within 60 days, 590 American POWs were freed to return home to the United States.

* * *

US Air Force EB-66 electronic warfare aircraft were occasionally employed to jam radar signals from the Russian Fan Song radar, which was used by the NVA to guide their SAM missiles. There were a limited number of EB-66 aircraft, so they were not used extensively.

* * *

A modified version of the single-engine F-105 fighter jet, known as the Wild Weasel, flew Operation Iron Hand missions to destroy SAM sites. They baited the enemy anti-aircraft defenses into targeting them. After a SAM was launched, the F-105s could detect and lock on to the Fan Song radar site and destroy it. The casualty rate for the Wild Weasel pilots was 63 percent (yes, you read that right), making it one of the riskiest missions in the air war.

GOOD-DEAL TRIPS

Good-deal trips for GIBs were available on a rotating basis. Selection was based on the amount of time a GIB had been in country. They were overnight trips that rotated between flying to an aircraft carrier or helicoptering to an Army observation post. Naturally, everyone wanted to go to the aircraft carrier. When my turn came, it was the Army observation post. I did not have to go, but I thought it might be interesting to see how the Army lived and worked out in the field.

My only interaction with the Army guys up to that point had been in passing at the base exchange. The most memorable encounters with the soldiers there were with those who were not old enough to buy liquor. Like beggars, they stood outside the BX trying to hand me money to buy them a bottle of booze. I initially accommodated them. Then I asked some of the guys back at the squadron how they handled that situation. Justification for not doing it was that young soldiers got boozed up before going out on a mission and ended up getting themselves killed. I found it sad and contradictory that our country could trust these young men to traipse through hostile territory carrying high-powered machine guns to engage a ferocious enemy, but it could not trust them with a bottle of liquor.

I was transported to the Army outpost in a Huey resupply helicopter. A gunner was stationed in the open doorway just in case there was a need to return any enemy groundfire. My visit had been prearranged through an Army/Air Force exchange program coordinator, so the Army troops were expecting me. Upon deplaning on the mountain top, I was greeted by the smell of a decomposing VC body that was dumped on the ground in a storage shed. The hot and humid Vietnam conditions enhanced the nasty odor. The Army guys told me they shot him when he was trying to invade the outpost. They were trying to figure out what to do with him.

The observation post was located on a mountain top that had steep escarpments. Its flat top was encircled with five-foot high sandbags. Several M-60 machine guns were positioned around the perimeter with their muzzles sticking out through openings in the sandbags. The Army guys let me fire off several rounds just for the heck of it.

The view from the mountain top was picturesque. There was a sense of tranquility at the base of this mountain. I was offered a pair of binoculars to view the Vietnamese agrarian culture with the *mama sans* and *papa sans* toiling in their rice paddies. They all wore the same style of conical hats, Chinese baggy trousers, and tunics. There was no powered machinery in the fields; it was all hand labor with a few ox-drawn carts.

One objective for these Army soldiers was to establish positive US relations with the local Vietnamese population. A road circled around the side of the mountain down to their village. The soldiers drove down the road in their two-and-a-half-ton truck (commonly referred to as a deuce and a half) followed by track vehicles with machine guns mounted on the rear. They visited with the elders and villagers who supposedly were friendly toward the Americans, at least in the daytime. I was not unhappy that they did not ask me to go along with them. After one night on that mountain top, I was ready to get back to my air-conditioned quarters at Danang. The Army guys were extremely cordial, but the accommodations were terrible.

My boss in the frag shop arranged another good-deal trip for me. It was a visit to 7th Air Force headquarters in Saigon, where the frag was developed. I was scheduled to fly there on a C-47 transport aircraft that regularly shuttled personnel and supplies between Danang and Tan Son Nhut Air Base. The C-47 was known as the gooney bird. It had been around for ages and there were several variations to it. It was used in WWII for paratroop drops during allied campaigns in Europe. In Vietnam, an AC-47 gunship was called *Puff the Magic Dragon*. An EC-47 electronic warfare version was put into service in Vietnam to spy on enemy activities in Laos. The civilian version of the C-47 was the DC-3 that was used extensively by airlines in the US. It was an old multipurpose airplane that should have been retired long before but the US Air Force lost 2,251 aircraft in the Vietnam War, so it was desperate for airplanes.

The flight from Danang to Tan Son Nhut AB started out okay. Then the noise level inside the aircraft got eerily quiet. The pilots were alerted to an engine warning light that mandated an engine shutdown. The C-47 flew good on one engine, so my flight continued on to Saigon.

I walked into downtown Saigon, which was packed with people and rundown shops. Bicycles, motor scooters, and small vehicles were everywhere. Rubble and garbage were strewn about. The hustle and bustle of locals doing their shopping made it appear that they were oblivious to the fact that a war was going on around them. Americans were generally taller than the Vietnamese and since I was wearing my flight suit, I was even more visible and drew some stares. I took along my movie camera and photographed four young Vietnamese men seated at an outdoor restaurant table drinking beer. They put on a little show for me, but I did not trust them, so I hastened my pace back to the Air Force headquarters building.

IN SUPPORT OF FRIENDLIES

During the monsoon season in Southeast Asia, the air-war missions from Danang focused on close-air support of friendly troops on the ground in South Vietnam. The ordnance loads included a mix of bombs and napalm. Napalm was dropped from the F-4 in a canister about the same size as a 500-pound bomb. When it impacted the ground, it exploded into a nasty fireball consisting of a flammable gel that splashed more than 500 feet. It was highly effective in controlling the advance of enemy troops. It must have been a dreadful sight for the enemy.

All our missions in South Vietnam were controlled by a FAC. The FAC was in communication with the friendlies to confirm their location. We always flew our bombing run-ins parallel to the location of the friendlies. Pilot placement of the pipper (crosshairs) on the target fore and aft was not always 100 percent accurate and sometimes a bomb momentarily hung up on the racks, causing it to release late and land long. We flew a shallow ten-degree dive angle to the target and pickled the bombs at an altitude of 1,000 feet. There was often a sense of urgency from the friendly military forces who wanted immediate and close placement of bombs due to a rapidly advancing enemy. We sometimes pressed below the 1,000-foot pickle altitude to get the bombs as close as possible to the friendlies.

The biggest threat to us was small arms gunfire, which was undetectable from inside our cockpit. It could be as hazardous as the larger antiaircraft guns. If a small arms bullet punctured a fuel tank or a hydraulic line, it could result in loss of the aircraft. Several thousand enemy troops in an NVA regiment all shooting at an F-4 at the same time filled the sky with lots of bullets.

I was flying a close air support mission with a top-notch AC—not that any were bad, but some were more enjoyable to fly with than others. A concentration of enemy troops in a mountain valley area was bearing down on friendlies and they needed help fast. The FAC marked the target and briefed us on the run-in heading, which was up a valley into a mountain. My AC and I confirmed our pickle altitude and estimated our capability to climb out of the valley and clear the top of the mountain. As a matter of procedure, the AC set his radar altimeter to 1,000 feet. If the aircraft descended below that height above ground, a warning light flashed on his dash. It was common to see this warning light on these types of missions. Even if the AC pickled at 1,000 feet, the aircraft would still be descending and losing altitude before establishing a positive rate of climb out of the dive. The radar altimeter only measured height straight down from the aircraft and not height above ground ahead of the aircraft so it was mostly useless when flying toward mountainous terrain. We found it best to rely on our judgement to maintain adequate terrain clearance.

On our run-in, I monitored altitude with reference to both the altimeter and outside visual cues. The AC pickled the bombs on my command and started a pull up. However, we had miscalculated how fast we closed on the rapidly approaching mountain ahead of us. It appeared that we hit some trees. I cannot explain what happened next. I do remember experiencing something that approximated what I have read as an out-of-body experience. Maybe it was the same feeling a person has when they are nearing an accidental death. I touched myself to confirm that I was still there. My AC was similarly alarmed by the close encounter with our demise. After we both regained our composure, we talked about it. At a speed of 500 knots, hitting anything on the ground normally resulted in disintegration of the aircraft. Some of the F-4s lost in the Vietnam War were likely the consequence of these types of demanding missions.

After we got back to Danang, the crew chief and I walked around our airplane, and pulled some twigs out of our pylons. The weird sensation that I experienced on that mission causes me to sometimes wonder if I am the same person today as I was before that happened.

THE SOB GAVE
ME AN EIGHT

L ife at Danang flying the F-4 was one of constantly living on the edge. I was young, fearless, and sometimes even thought maybe I was invincible. Perhaps a better term would be cocky. By now, I had a lot of combat experience and could take charge in nearly any flying situation.

At times, it would have been easy to get down in the dumps and go to my room and sulk. Instead, I stepped out of my character and developed close relationships with the guys. I was comfortable with my social abilities and was well respected by fellow aviators at Danang. I went over to the squadron building and drank beer, played darts, and got into card games. In my first blackjack game, I played against three guys, one of whom was a major who was also my reporting official. I bet a small amount of money. Then I started winning, so I doubled my bet and won again, then again, and again. I was taking this major's money and was starting to feel guilty about it, so I put all my money in the pot hoping that I would lose; but as luck would have it, I won again. I worried that my reporting official would somehow seek revenge against me for taking his money, so I decided to bow out of the game. I tried to give him his money back, but he refused. He was not a happy guy and I suspect that it was not because he lost money to me or was outsmarted, but rather it was because he lost to someone who had beginner's luck.

As my reporting official, he would write my first officer evaluation report (OER). The OER rating was a big factor in determining if I would get promoted to captain. OERs were part of an officer's permanent personnel record and remained in Air Force files for an officer's entire career.

Raters often asked ratees to provide bullet statements that could be used in their OER. One pilot had a sense of humor and was calling it quits in the Air Force after leaving Vietnam, so he gave these statements to his rater:

1. Faster than a speeding bullet.
2. More powerful than a locomotive.
3. Able to leap tall buildings in a single bound.

The rating scale on an OER was one thru nine, with nine being the highest. Personal ratings were supposed to be kept private, but the GIBs talked amongst ourselves, so I knew the ratings that my cohorts received on their OERs. The Air Force OER rating system was quite inflated. All other GIBs in my squadron got the highest rating of nine.

The major writing my OER was the same AC who I flew with on the ill-fated Cambodia mission; and he was the same major who I always pulled the stick back on during bombing runs because he pressed below the pickle altitude. We were not exactly on the best of terms.

He handed me my OER and it was not a nine; it was an eight. My immediate thought was:

The son of a bitch gave me an eight.

Air Force regulations required him to review it with me. He must have detected the look of disappointment on my face, so he tried to explain his logic for giving me an eight. He considered an eight to be the top of his personal rating scale for anyone who was getting their first OER in the Air Force. There would be room to demonstrate improvement over time. It was not a very convincing argument. I was doing a great job in a combat zone, was putting my butt on the line for my country, and now I was going to be competing for promotion against other pilots who had no combat experience and who would probably have a nine on their OER. I felt like I had been screwed, so in response, I made it known to the squadron scheduling officer that I never wanted to fly with that guy again.

* * *

The intensity of the air war did not lessen in late 1970; only the area of focus shifted. Except for an occasional mission into Laos or Cambodia, my remaining missions were against targets in South Vietnam. Some of the most heavily defended targets were imbedded in the border area between Laos and South Vietnam, known as the A Shau Valley. The rugged valley was a narrow twenty-five-mile-long gap in the mountains with 6,800-foot steep peaks on both sides. Most of the Ho Chi Minh trails from the mountainous regions of Laos funneled into South Vietnam through this valley. It was a hotly contested area and was the setting for some of the war's bloodiest operations because of its strategic importance to the North Vietnamese for transporting their supplies to the Viet Cong. Underground NVA bunkers along the mountainous sides of the valley harbored enemy 23mm and 37mm antiaircraft guns. US military ground troops worked the area, and F-4 pilots sat alert at Danang, ready to scramble in support of them. There was some consolation in knowing that if we had to punch out, there was at least a chance that we might come down into the hands of nearby friendly troops.

One-room schoolhouse—1949

Author at 11 years of age with 4-H steer

Ma and Dad—
Circa 1950's

Farmhouse—Circa 1950's

Farm buildings

Horse Barn, Cattle Barn, Corncrib, Grainery, and Shed

Barn, Silo, Corncrib, Chicken Coop, Manure Spreader, Milk Cans, and Swill Barrels

Church in the country

Author's wife and son in front of T-37 and T-38—1968

Author and T-38—1969

Gunfighter F-4E
at Da Nang AB,
Vietnam, loaded
with bombs

366 TFW Patch with
mascot, "Spook"

The author's one
and only parade

To the Men of the 48th Fighter Interceptor Squadron
With appreciation and best wishes,

Richard Nixon

F-106 and President's airplane—1971

Randy, Sandy, Paul, and George—1991

PART SIX

GOING HOME

By October, my time at Danang was thankfully short. I was in the double-digit fidgets, meaning less than 100 days to go, so it appeared that the end was in sight. I anxiously awaited notification on my next assignment.

Personnel records for every officer were maintained at the Air Force Personnel Center located at Randolph AFB, Texas. One important record in an officer's file was his dream sheet. An officer could indicate what they wanted to do in the Air Force and where they wanted to do it. It was called a dream sheet because you specified the assignment you wanted; the Air Force sent you wherever they needed you.

There were Air Force bases in a variety of places throughout the world. Some were in tropical locations such as Hickam AB, Hawaii, or Homestead AFB, Florida. Others were in cold and snowy Billings, Montana; Thule, Greenland; or Minot, North Dakota. Pilots indicated their aircraft preference on the dream sheet. You could ask for an F-106 fighter interceptor aircraft but end up getting a C-130 cargo aircraft. It was rare, but it was a possibility. If a pilot was in a fighter aircraft track, he usually stayed in that track unless he specified otherwise. Many F-4 pilots intended to make the Air Force a career for twenty years, so they wanted to stay in fighters. Others had enough of the Air Force after Vietnam and wanted to pursue a career in the airlines, so they preferred something a little more sedate, like a Boeing KC135 air refueling aircraft, which had the same systems as the Boeing 707 commercial airliners.

It was smart to keep the dream sheet up to date. If it was not on a dream sheet, then it was a crapshoot what you got. Nobody from the personnel center was going to call you and ask what you wanted to fly or where you wanted to go. I specified two choices on my dream sheet. My second choice was to upgrade to the front seat of the F-4. It would be an easy conversion since I was already familiar with the aircraft. Problem was that if I got it, I would probably be sent back to Southeast Asia. I could maybe get a base in Thailand instead of Vietnam but with the slow rate of progress toward ending the Vietnam War, I would probably end up flying missions back into Laos and North Vietnam. Even more importantly, another year away from Sandy and our son did not seem too appealing.

I decided to go far out on my dream sheet and list the F-106 as my first choice. The F-106 was a sleek looking, high speed, single-seat, single-engine, fighter/interceptor aircraft. It was nicknamed the *delta dart* because it had swept-back, triangle shaped wings and an elongated fuselage that resembled a dart. It was fast, even faster than an F-4; it could get up to a speed of Mach 2.4. Pilots facetiously commented it was so maneuverable that you could fly up your own ass with it. During the Cold War, our country's military had to be on constant alert for a potential airborne attack from Russia. The F-106 mission was air defense to intercept and, if necessary, shoot down invading enemy aircraft. I liked the idea of not having to throw my rear end at the ground on bombing missions.

The Air Force had spent a lot of money on my training, so they expected something in return. I had four years remaining on my commitment to the Air Force, and I had every intention of making the Air Force a career. From a financial standpoint, the Air Force offered good fringe benefits, such as housing allowance, per diem, subsistence allowance, combat pay, separation allowance, medical care for me and my family, base exchange privileges, and thirty days annual leave. It was not a bad career if you could put up with some BS. If I stayed for twenty years, I could retire and get 50 percent of my pay.

A couple of weeks before my DEROS from Vietnam, I got my next assignment. They evidently looked at my dream sheet and assigned me an F-106. One week prior to my DEROS in November, I was scheduled to fly my last mission. Of course, it was over Laos because the rainy season had ended and the air war had resumed. I was scheduled to fly with an AC who was also on his last mission. We both had strong survival instincts and were not going to push the envelope. After successfully flying 200 missions, it would be awful to get shot down on the last one. As expected, the North Vietnamese unloaded their usual fireworks, and gave me a send-off more spectacular than any reception I would get when I got back home in the states. I breathed a sigh of relief when we exited the Laotian airspace one last time. I never wanted to see that place again.

After landing at Danang, guys from the squadron were all waiting in the bread truck and maintenance pick-up trucks. They corralled a fire truck and an ambulance. I knew in advance what was in store for me so I prearranged for one of my buddies to use my movie camera to film it so I could show it back home to anybody who cared.

We shut down the engines on our beloved F-4 in the de-arming area. I could not wait for the crew chief to hook up the ladder to my cockpit rail. Instead, I threw off my shoulder harness, jumped onto the wing of the aircraft, slipped, and bounced off the leading edge of the aircraft pylon with my butt before falling to the tarmac. My tailbone hurt something terrible, but this was not a time to think about pain. I tried to get my G suit off but only got one leg unzipped before they doused me with water from a fire hose. After some hopping around on my free leg and jostling with the guys for control of the fire hose, I was hoisted into the back of a pick-up truck. They had a sign attached to the top of the truck. *Lt. George Kohn–201 Missions*. The small gaggle of vehicles made its way around the flight line with lights flashing, horns blaring, and guys hooting and hollering. This was my send-off from Danang.

I got my belongings packed and ready to ship home. I came to Vietnam with just a duffle bag, but now I had stereo equipment, audio tapes, and records. The Air Force would pay for shipping them, but I first had to get them boxed. The Air Force had established an informal arrangement with some Vietnamese locals in Dog Patch village. It was my responsibility to take the items to them and to pay them for packaging. They then delivered the items to a container ship. The Air Force only accepted responsibility for my belongings after the items arrived at the ship.

I heard that it was a good idea to keep an eye on your stuff until it was loaded onto the truck and destined for the ship. Packages usually made it to the ship, but there were some that only made it to the Vietnamese back room. On my trips to China Beach, I spotted many Vietnamese shacks outside the base that had nice stereo equipment on the shelves. I strapped on my holster and .38 revolver to display a show of intimidation to the packers. Later, I got to thinking about that action. Would I really have used the revolver on a Vietnamese human being over the theft of a piece of stereo equipment?

* * *

Looking back, I had a good relationship with all the pilots in my squadron and in the frag shop. We had good times, and we had sad times. We shared a lot of stories and we shared danger. I knew that I was leaving behind great guys, some of whom would possibly not go home. Some were in double digits and others were relatively new to Vietnam. They had to stay behind and fight this danged war. I had a mixture of joy and sadness. I would miss them.

It would be exactly 365 days since I left home in the States. I boarded the DC-8 airliner out of Danang that was packed with servicemen returning from the war in Vietnam. As I settled in my seat, I quietly went into a deep trance. Am I really going home? This was the moment I had so anxiously awaited since arriving one year prior. Thoughts about the previous year flashed through my mind at a million miles a minute. I fell asleep and did not wake up until the flight descended for landing. The coastline of California was beautiful, but I still had an awful sensation that I was being shot at. That sensation persisted for a long time, occasionally cropping up even late in my aviation career.

After deplaning at Travis AFB, I took a shuttle from the military base over to the civilian airport in San Francisco. I had reservations for a flight back home that required a connection through Chicago. Since the Air Force was paying for my flight, I had to travel in military uniform. I had heard about the reception I could expect. True to character, long-haired, druggy-looking creeps were waiting in San Francisco with *baby killer* signs and cheeks gyrating to broadcast their intention to direct spit and snot at returning veterans. I took a great deal of pride in my military uniform and did not want it dishonored, so I picked up the pace and jogged to my connecting flight. I ran behind airport columns to get to the gate for the final leg of my flight home. Welcome home from service to your country, George.

Sandy, Paul, Ma, and Dad met me at the airport. I had thirty days to rest before reporting for my F-106 assignment. I attended my old church on the first Sunday home and was grateful that parishioners talked to me and displayed happiness that I had safely returned. I anticipated interest from other folks in the community about my Vietnam experiences, and mentally prepared to speak at local VFW and Legion meetings, town council meetings, to high school students, or even to chatter at the taverns about Vietnam. Over the years, I awaited an invitation to participate in hometown parades to represent Vietnam Veterans. My parade at Danang was my one and only parade.

I left isolation in my hometown to report for my assignment in the F-106. Few guys in my squadron had been to Vietnam. I assumed, much to my chagrin, that sitting in an air defense alert shack alone with another guy would stimulate some discussion about Vietnam. My hopes dissipated when I came to the realization that people in this country did not give a crap about the experiences of a Vietnam Veteran. I had been part of a military establishment promoted by the media as being responsible for my country losing a war. The silent treatment from the populace about Vietnam was equally as powerful on my mental health as any spoken words.

PONTIFICATION

According to the *Cambridge English Dictionary*, pontification means "to write and give your opinion about something as if you knew everything about it."

While I was never adept at verbalization, I liked to write. Writing gave me time to formulate and refine my deep-seated thoughts and opinions, so here goes. After serving my country honorably, I believe that I have earned the right to pontificate (okay, so it is a big word, but I like it). I have concerns about the treatment of Vietnam Veterans in this country, both during and after the war. I believe that we must learn from this chapter in our country's history and never let such disrespect toward our military personnel ever happen again.

Politicians from the Vietnam era should be remembered for failing to espouse a clearly defined objective in Vietnam. Throughout the war, our government seemed incapable of providing accurate information to the media and to the public. Cowardly political incompetence was evidenced by a failure to provide public support for returning military personnel, and by abandoning them to the whims of the media and vocal dissidents.

Sensational negatives coming out of the media unquestionably influenced public opinion against Vietnam Veterans. One privileged American traitor was heroized by the media while sitting on a North Vietnamese antiaircraft gun in Hanoi shooting off her mouth about US military atrocities in Vietnam. There was the widely circulated photo of a

South Vietnamese General executing a Viet Cong prisoner during the Tet Offensive and it earned a Pulitzer for the photographer. A photo of a naked little girl running from an errant napalm attack was broadcast nationwide. Newspapers boldly displayed pictures of the Kent State killings of four student protestors by the National Guard. There was the perpetual drama of the William Calley trial and the My Lai massacre by an Army platoon that had lost more than forty men from repeated attacks by the Viet Cong, and the constant ritual of reporting body counts to emphasize the disastrous nature of the war. Military ineptitude was reportedly responsible for seventy Americans killed in the battle for Hamburger Hill. There was widespread media coverage of the bombing of the Army Mathematics Research Center and Sterling Hall by anti-Vietnam War radicals. The mastermind of the bombing spent seven years in jail; two of his cohorts spent three years in jail for killing a researcher and causing massive destruction of public property. One newspaper praised their actions. There was the derisive music coming out of the Woodstock festival, the hoopla surrounding the trial of the Chicago Seven anti-war radicals, and widespread media coverage of the collapse of morale, interracial tensions, drug abuse, and disciplinary problems among American troops. It went on and on and on. Then a reputable anchor on nationwide television stated that the conflict (emphasis that it was a conflict, not a war) was "mired in stalemate." Richard Nixon commented that "our worst enemy seems to be the press." Adding to the insults, the day after he was inaugurated on January 21, 1977, President Carter issued an unconditional pardon to 100,000 draft dodgers and deserters who had fled to Canada. Upon returning home, he promised them an open-arms reunion. With this preponderance of mockery and ridicule toward the military, how could there be any doubt that society would assume a negative outlook toward anyone who participated in that war?

There seemed to be minimal discussion of the positive attributes and devoted efforts of Vietnam military personnel. Those Army troops on that mountain top were surrounded by infestations of enemy Viet Cong troops but they still pursued their mission of establishing positive relations with Vietnamese locals. F-105 pilots gave their lives or years of freedom to avoid flying over sensitive areas while en route to bombing missions over Hanoi. There were the heroic efforts to rescue Boxer 22, the troops who gave their MRE candy to Vietnamese children, the humane treatment of enemy POWs in our military hospitals, and the numerous musicians and performers who risked their lives to put on a USO show for the troops. There had to be an endless number of good deeds that our United States personnel did in Vietnam, but they were not newsworthy items. Did those stories contradict the negative theme that was being propagated about the US military involvement in the Vietnam War?

The media unquestionably swayed public opinion against veterans who had placed their lives on the line for all the right reasons. As a result, I received zero respect for my efforts to keep our country free. I was shunned for contributing to an unpopular war that went down in history as a *loss*. I am now going to be very straightforward. I was deeply disappointed in our society for its lack of respect, not just toward me, but toward all returning Vietnam military personnel.

Yes, I admit that I was somewhat bitter about all of this. I now hope that we have learned a lesson from the Vietnam War era and that we, as a country, cannot and should not tolerate name calling, biases, nor animosity toward our dedicated military personnel, nor, for that matter, toward anyone in our society.

The Vietnam War was (and still is) being publicized as a loss for the Unites States of America. Some might argue that Ho Chi Minh achieved his objective when the outcome was the eventual unification of North and South Vietnam. We must also remember that Ho Chi Minh was a communist puppet of the Soviet Union and China. One way to look at the outcome would be to consider what the world would be like today if we had not fought that war. Remember the domino theory – how one country after another would topple if the communists were not stopped in Vietnam? People in this country must understand that the alternative to democracy was not acceptable in Vietnam, in any country in Southeast Asia, nor in the United States of America.

By fighting the Vietnam War, we deterred the spread of communism throughout the world. Even if we concede the premise that we did not win the war to maintain the sovereignty of South Vietnam, we sure put up a heck of a fight, and maybe gave the communists something to think about before they tried to march in and take over another country. Here is a call to historians. Rewrite the history books, but this time get the analysis right.

I believe that I can speak for other Vietnam veterans in stating that the contributions of our Vietnam veterans to protect our democracy was a commendable effort for our country. Next time a citizen of the United States of America has the opportunity to select a career, a place of worship, a leader, to express a viewpoint in a respectful manner, to have a choice of news sources or whatever other freedoms they now enjoy, it should be remembered that those are privileges that a Vietnam veteran put his life on the line for so that we all can still live in a democracy. Vietnam veterans stopped the spread of communism in Southeast Asia and preserved the freedoms that we take for granted but so dearly cherish. No Vietnam veteran I know needs to be remembered as a hero, but they would sure be grateful to be respected for their contribution to our country.

Many Vietnam veterans still carry a heavy, hidden burden from that war. It is reflected in veteran homelessness, disability, disease, disorder, and probably many other insidious ways. That burden must often be shared with millions of loved ones of those Veterans. The stress and strain of separation during the war and the uncertainties imposed on wives, husbands, parents, family members, and friends took a heavy toll on relationships. Family members deserve a great deal of praise and respect for persevering throughout that agonizing time, not knowing if their loved one would return. When they did return, there was the uncertainty about whether the person who came home was the same person who they knew and loved before he or she went to Vietnam. Then, to endure the stories about their loved ones being spit on and chastised for serving their country is unfathomable. I am truly blessed to have Sandy as my wife, for my two sons Paul and Randy, and am deeply grateful for their unwavering moral support.

Fifty-eight thousand two hundred and twenty Americans gave their lives in Vietnam to defend our freedoms. Over three hundred thousand were wounded. I was merely one of the 2.4 million Americans who served in Vietnam. My story is not unique. Many great warriors came out of the Vietnam War; some of them accomplished amazing feats. I did none of that. I did not accomplish anything extraordinary in Vietnam other than to do my job and to survive.

Over 1,000,000 North Vietnamese died in that war. On numerous missions, I had dropped bombs on moving vehicles, gun emplacements, and enemy concentrations; I was certainly responsible for some of those deaths. I offer my condolences to the families of those brave warriors. Supposedly it was okay to kill another human under the guise of a justifiable war. I pray that things will be right for me with my God on judgment day.

My story cannot be complete without one final comment. I overcame many obstacles to become a fighter pilot, but there was this constant reminder that it was not right that I selfishly take all the credit for it. It was highly unusual that a farm kid with my background could be so fortunate in life as to be rewarded with the opportunity to reach such lofty goals. Was it just my doing? Was it possible that, by myself, I could pick up and leave the farm and with no college preparation, get a college degree, become a pilot in the United States Air Force, fly fighter jets, and survive a nasty war? Obviously, there was a guiding hand vectoring me to my destiny. I will always be eternally grateful for God's guidance in my life.

FINAL NOTE

My active duty flying career in the Air Force ended when I encountered another bout of severe abdominal pain. This time the pain was on the opposite side from the previous occurrence when I was in college. Bilateral kidney stones were a grounding condition. I joined the Air Force Reserve and was eventually permitted a return to flying in multi-crew C-130 transport airplanes. I was privileged to continue serving my country in the United States Air Force for thirty-two years.

The Vietnam era was a dark chapter in American history for many veterans. It is encouraging to now observe that respect for military personnel has become an integral part of our society. One example for me took place after I retired from flying in 2003. I returned to organic farming like Dad used to do, to emphasize the hazards of farm chemicals that caused the death of my dear sister in Arizona. I was selling bedding plants from our farm at the local farmer's market. With a long white beard and dirt on my pants, I was certainly not a military-looking person from my appearance.

I was somewhat startled when an elderly lady whom I had never met before came up to me and said: "You're a Vietnam veteran, aren't you?"

Uncertain about why she was asking and not sure where this conversation was heading, I somewhat sheepishly responded: "Yes ma'am, I am."

"Thank you for your service," she said.

Trying to be somewhat suave and struggling to find the right words despite some welling emotions, all I could think of was: "Thank you, ma'am."

We are truly blessed to live in a great country. I hope that my story accurately and appropriately represents the contributions and sacrifices of our Vietnam veterans. To them, and to all our veterans, thank you for your service. And to all of you readers, my deepest gratitude for letting me tell my story.

With a humble heart—thank you,
Col. George W. Kohn, USAFR (Ret.)

NUGGETS

Be your world big or small; know His hand is in control
Your destiny is yet to be; your end will tell the last journey
Let it be, oh let it be; a hark to all, for all to see
A guiding hand led you my son; you are His much beloved one
Open your eyes humble peasantry; open your eyes and you will see
God works in you; God's works in me. **—Anonymous**

"Yea though I walk **through** the **valley** of the shadow of **death**, I shall
fear no evil: for thou art with me, thy rod and thy staff, they comfort
me. You prepare a table before me in the presence of my enemies."
—Psalm 23:4

"Believe with all your heart that you will do what you were made to do."
—Orison Swett Marden

"But by the grace of God I am what I am, and his grace to me was not
without effect."*—1 Corinthians 1 5:10*

"We are not given a good life or a bad life. We are given life. And it's up to us to make it good or bad."—*Ward Foley*

"And we know that in all things God works for the good of those who love him, who have been called according to his purpose."
—*Romans 8:28*

ACRONYMS AND SUCH

AAA—Antiaircraft Artillery

AB—Airbase

ABCCC—Airborne Battlefield Command and Control Center

AC—Aircraft Commander

ADF—Automatic Direction Finder

AFM—Air Force Manual

AFOQT—Air Force Officer Qualification Test

BDA—Bomb Damage Assessment

Bingo fuel—Minimum fuel needed to return to Danang

Bogey—Radar contact on an aerial target

BUFF—Big Ugly Fat Fellows

CBPO—Central Base Personnel Office

CBU—Cluster Bomb Unit

CIA—Central Intelligence Agency

Clicks—Kilometers

DEROS—Date Estimated Return from Overseas

DME—Distance Measuring Equipment

DMZ—Demilitarized Zone

DNIF—Duty Not Including Flying

EGT—Exhaust Gas Temperature

FAA—Federal Aviation Administration

FAC—Forward Air Controller

FBO—Fixed Base Operation

FCF—Functional Check Flight

GCA—Ground Controlled Approach

GIB—Guy in Back

IFR—Instrument Flight Rules

INS—Inertial Navigation System

JINK—Rapid Aircraft Maneuver

KIA—Killed in Action

KNOTS—Nautical miles per hour

MACH—Velocity relative to the speed of sound

MERS—Multiple Ejection Racks

MIA—Missing in Action

MIG—A Russian Made Aircraft

MRE—Meal Ready to Eat

NVA—North Vietnamese Army

OER—Officer Evaluation Report

OTS —Officer Training School

Pickle—Bomb release

PJ—Para Jumper

PLF—Parachute Landing Fall

POW—Prisoner of War

PRF—Pulse Recurring Frequency

PTO—Power Takeoff

R&R—Rest and Relaxation

Ret.—Retired

RHAW—Radar Homing and Warning

ROTC—Reserve Officer Training Corp

SAM—Surface to Air Missile

SAR—Search and Rescue

TFW—Tactical Fighter Wing

TOT—Time Over Target

UFO—Unidentified Flying Objects

UHF—Ultra High Frequency

USO—United Service Organization

VC—Viet Cong

VHF—Very High Frequency

WRCS—Weapons Release Computer System

ZPU—A Russian made Antiaircraft Gun

ACKNOWLEDGMENTS

My deepest appreciation goes to my loving wife Sandy for hanging in there with me for fifty-six years. To my two sons Paul (friend, Victoria) and Randy (wife, Tanya), I am proud of you for many reasons, including your military service to our country. To my three beautiful granddaughters, Savannah, Lexi, and Nikkia, whom I love with all my heart, you unknowingly inspired me to write my story. To my family and friends, thank you for hanging in there with me when my mind was out in space. Thank you to the kind folks at Köehler Books for your superb expertise in getting this story published. A very special thank you to those who have written endorsements. To my beta readers, Sammi Goldberg, Brikitta Hairston, Dustin N, and Steve Amsden, I am grateful for your great feedback. I am thankful for everyone else who played a role in bringing this story to fruition. And to you, the reader, I want to convey my sincerest appreciation.

I would be honored if you would write a review of this book on Amazon. Sign in to your Amazon account, select *Vector to Destiny*, scroll down to *Customer Reviews*, and add your comments. Thank you.

Perhaps some of you have had similar experiences where there is clear evidence that God has directed your destiny in life. If so, I would like to hear about them or any other thoughts you may have on the book. Please visit my website at: www.gwkohnauthor.com or email me at gwkohnauthor@gmail.com.

CPSIA information can be obtained
at www.ICGtesting.com
Printed in the USA
LVHW091346161120
671823LV00005B/78